Ideas and techniques for fabric design

IDEAS AND TECHNIQUES
FOR FABRIC DESIGN

LYNDA FLOWER

Senior Lecturer in charge of textile design
Berkshire College of Art and Design

Longman   London and New York

Longman Group Limited
Longman House, Burnt Mill, Harlow
Essex CM20 2JE, England
Associated companies throughout the world

*Published in the United States of America
by Longman Inc., New York*

© Longman Group Limited 1986

First published 1986

British Library Cataloguing in Publication Data

Flower, Lynda
  Ideas and techniques for fabric design.
  1. Textile design
  I. Title
  677′.022   TS1475
  ISBN 0-582-41312-5

Set in Linotron 10/11 pt Plantin
Produced by Longman Group (FE) Limited
Printed in Hong Kong

Contents

Acknowledgements

We are grateful to the following for permission to reproduce copyright material:

David Anderson Gallery, New York/Richard Anuszkiewicz for our Fig. 1.3(a); Michael Brennand-Wood for our Fig. 1.1(b); Trustees of the British Museum for our Figs. 7.3, 8.14 and 8.15; Pauline Burbidge for our Fig. 1.5(a); Leo Castelli Gallery, New York for our Fig. 1.5(b); Patrick Caulfield for our Fig. 2.4(c); Conde Naste publications for our Fig. 1.3(b), photographer Henry Clarke; Noel Dyrenforth/collection of Professor Yoko Tajima, Tokyo for our Fig. 8.11; Alan Flux for our Fig. 2.7; Sam Gilliam for our Fig. 1.4(b); Ernst Haas for our Fig. 2.5(c); Diana Harrison for our Figs. 9.14(a), 9.14(b) and 9.15; Holly Solomon Gallery, Morton G. Neumann Family Collection/Kim MacConnel for our Fig. 1.2(b); By courtesy of the Trustees, The National Gallery, London our Fig. 2.4(a); Natural History Museum, London; E. Paolozzi for our Fig. 1.2(a); Royal College of Art, London, Furniture School for our Fig. 2.2(b) piece made by Ron Lenthall, designed by Michael Gurney; Science Museum, London for our Figs. 1.4(a) and 2.16; Scottish National Gallery, Edinburgh for our Fig. 2.1; Collection of Professor Yoko Tajima for our Fig. 8.11; Tate Gallery, London/John Dugger for our Fig. 1.1(a); Tate Gallery, London/E. Paolozzi for our Fig. No 1.2(a); Tate Gallery, London/Richard Anuszkiewicz for our Fig. 1.3(a); Tate Gallery, London/Patrick Caulfield for our Fig. 2.4(c); By courtesy of the Board of Trustees of the Victoria and Albert Museum for our Figs. 1.6, 2.3(a), 2.3(b), 2.3(c), 2.3(d), 2.3(e), 2.3(f), 2.4(b), 3.3, 3.7, 3.11(b), 4.1(a), 4.1(b), 8.1 and 8.3; Malcolm White for our Fig. 2.8(c) and Warner and Sons Ltd. for our Fig. 4.1(c).

To June and Pat, Joan and Maud

Introduction

Imagine three people: 'A' is a talented and confident would-be designer. She has no trouble producing original and striking designs on paper, but has little knowledge of how her designs could be produced, either by traditional or by industrial methods.

'B' is an enthusiastic amateur working, perhaps, from home. He has spent time mastering various techniques, but flounders when it comes to 'design'. He simply does not know where to begin, and so falls back on familiar motifs, and puts all his efforts into developing time-consuming technical processes. The results are often breathtakingly intricate, but disappointing – somehow not quite original.

'C' on the other hand has developed both sides of textile design. She may, or may not, eventually produce the fabrics herself, but she understands the potential of the techniques that are used to produce them and the ways in which these techniques can affect her work. Her designs are enriched by this knowledge, and her technical mastery is equalled by the standard of her design.

When working in craft areas these two aspects should complement each other perfectly, and in this book I make the point that an understanding of technique and good design cannot successfully exist one without the other. If a craft is pursued without any sensitivity to design it becomes stale and empty, and the designer who ignores technical processes is depriving herself or himself of a rich source of inspiration.

'Design' is no secret; the elements of design are all around us, and are available to be used by all. I have tried to show what these elements are, and how they can be used with reference to various techniques.

The techniques themselves are less esoteric. They are easy to learn, and can be broken down into definite stages. They can be freely investigated by the amateur, yet developed to high levels by the more experienced.

It is this aspect of textile art and craft that makes it so

rewarding: it is an area in which there is room for the artist, the commerical designer, the craftsperson, and the amateur. Each has something to offer it, and it offers each of them something different.

METRIC/IMPERIAL CONVERSION TABLE

Metric measurements used in this book, with imperial equivalents

Metric measurements	Imperial equivalents
Length	
1 millimetre (m)	0.039 in
1 centimetre (cm)	0.393 in
1 metre (m)	1.093 yd
Volume	
1 millilitre (m)	0.061 cu. in
1 litre (l)*	0.219 gal
Mass	
1 gram (g)	0.035 oz
1 kilogram (kg)	2.204 lb

*Unit abbreviation not used in this book.

CHAPTER 1

Art, design, and craft

For the past 30 or so years we have witnessed the blurring of the edges that separated the 'fine' arts from the 'applied' arts. Since the 1960s the boundaries of acceptability that we have set ourselves, and inherited, have been pushed further and further away. With the *nouveau riche* pop stars and working-class entrepreneurs of the 1960s a completely new type of patron was born, who had artistic inclinations of his own, and the money to indulge them. Pop stars and pop artists became cult figures as much for their life styles as for their work. By living out the intriguing personae that they created for themselves, the mingling of pop art and pop music came about, and found its expression in the multi-media explosions of light and colour seen in the psychedelic pop concerts of the era.

As, always, the dictates of style and fashion filtered through all the visual arts, linking them together through cross-pollination. As barriers were rapidly breached due to the use of new media, and a new approach to old media, it became less necessary or desirable to differentiate between various art forms.

A whole new element of fun came into art at this time, with Claes Oldenbourg's giant hamburgers, soft typewriters, and flaccid 'drainpipes', all made out of fabrics. In the 1960s fabric finally broke free from its frame, and materials such as flax, felt, and rope were used to create objects that were a cross between painting, sculpture, and tapestry.

We are indebted to these pop artists, as they have paved the way for artists working today who feel free to use fabric and paint in any way they choose, without having to categorise their work (see Fig. 1.1).

This increasing artistic freedom has left the layman in a confusing position as ideas and media merge in the art world. He sees fabrics in the stores that look like paintings, paintings in the galleries that look like curtains, and 'hand made objects' that were once part of everyday living elevated to the status of art forms.

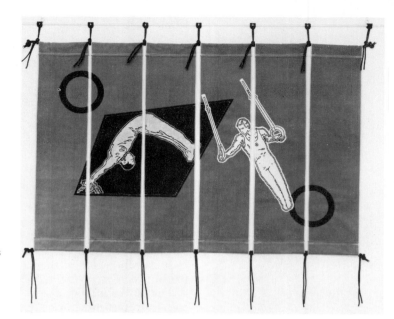

Fig. 1.1 Thanks to the pop artists of the 1960s we no longer expect artists to limit themselves to certain media.
(a) 'Sports banner', by John Dugger, 1980

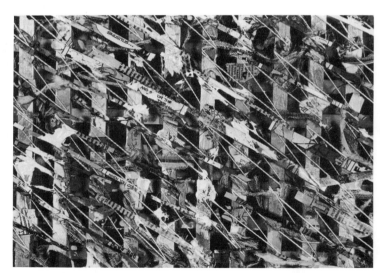

(b) 'White crayola', by Michael Brennand-Wood, 1978

In the early days before totally abstract painting became commonplace, the man in the street knew that he could see pattern where it belonged – in the shops. Bought by the metre and hung at a window it was without pretensions, undemanding and attractive. Yet when abstract painting was

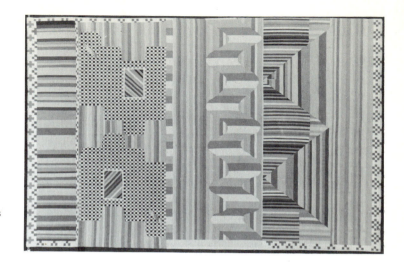

Fig. 1.2 The general public has always found it hard to accept abstract 'decorative' paintings as 'Art'.
(a) 'Tapestry' by Edvardo Paolozzi

(b) 'Baton rouge', by Kim MacConnel

hung in art galleries, or sold for very high prices it made demands that the man in the street could not meet. He preferred to see artists' work plagiarised by designers if it meant that pattern kept its place.

The fine arts have often proved too much of a 'gift' for designers to ignore, and thus it is that we periodically see art diminished but popularised as it was in the 1960s during the 'Op art' and 'Mondrian' crazes when the works of Bridget Riley, Victor Vasarely and Mondrian were 'borrowed' and regurgitated by fabric designers.

Fig. 1.3 Pattern: where does it belong?
(a) 'Division of intensity' painting by Richard Anuszkiewicz, 1964
(b) 'Hypnotical illusions'. Stripes designed by Getulio Alviani for Marucelli of Milan, 1965, photographer Henry Clarke, reproduced by courtesy of Naste Publications Ltd.

At about this time exciting new fabric-printing techniques that were being developed enabled effects that previously could only have been produced on paper, to be printed on cloth. This led to the intriguing game of 'putting famous paintings into repeat', and even if it did mean that a work of art was reduced to a blur of unamusing blandness, it enabled each one of us to buy our own Vermeer or Leonardo Da Vinci printed on unending yards of polyester. Art reduced to pattern was acceptable, to us pattern elevated to art was not (Fig. 1.3).

Even we who have had an 'art education' like to keep things where they belong, nurturing our own prejudices and snobbery about what is, and what is not, art. We draw clear lines in our minds, depending upon where and how we view an artist's work, and what we know of the intentions of the artist. A painting released from its frame does not necessarily become a curtain; we know it is not a curtain because it is hanging in an art gallery. Were it draped across a bed, or hung at a window the story would be a different one (see Fig. 1.4). Similarly, a craft work can be turned into an art work by the application of paint by one whom we accept as an artist. Which we prefer – art or craft – depends upon our own personal taste (see Fig. 1.5).

Fig. 1.4 'Art' is where we see it.
(a) Part of the first moon landing parachute, Photo:
(b) 'Carousel form II', A free-hanging painted canvas by Sam Gilliam. Exhibited at the Jefferson Place Gallery, Washington DC

(c) Shop curtains

Fig. 1.5   Art and craft.
(a) 'Kaleidoscope variations'.
Quilt, by Pauline Burbidge
(b) 'Bed'. Combine painting, by
Robert Rauschenberg (Photo
Courtesy of Leo Castelli Gallery,
New York)

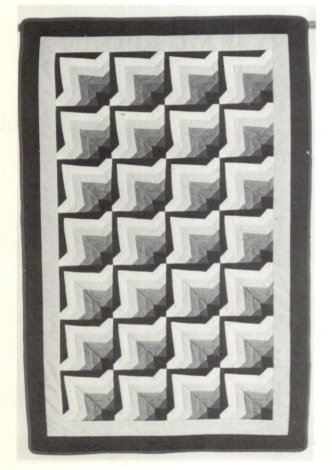

Crafts have always been the poor relation of art, acceptable in art galleries only if justified by an 'artist'. Yet the position of modern crafts is becoming more important due to the fact that many artists and designers are working in the craft areas, bringing in new ideas and fresh approaches to traditional materials. This, coupled with the influence of such bodies as the Crafts Council, the Design Centre, and the Victoria and Albert Museum in London (not to mention equally influential institutes in other countries) is leading to a fresh evaluation of crafts.

Commercial textile design is another matter. By its nature it has its roots firmly in industry and commerce, and has only tenuous links with art or craft. With the notable exception of William Morris, who managed to combine craft and commerce, few artists have worked in the field of commercial textile design. With the advent of screen printing several artists became interested in printed textiles (see Fig. 1.6), but the reproduction, and often the reduction in scale did not, in general, suit their work, and they did not explore the textile media further.

As time has passed, and the total industrialisation of the industry has taken place, the two sides of textile design have become less and less reconcilable. Only small private companies with their limited finances and facilities can hope to keep design and production together.

Fig. 1.6 'Cette parade sauvage', by Fernand Léger. Léger was one of the first artists who became interested in screen printing on fabric

So where does this leave the textile student of today? As you become more familiar with the field in which you work you will see the two sides of printed textiles recede from each other. The commerical designer works within the broadest confines, yet is still limited by the vagaries of fashion and mass taste. He must work for and understand the most sophisticated equipment, yet know that once his design is sold he will have no further control over the development of the final product. The craftsman, on the other hand, as the designer and creator of the final product works solely within the limitations of the media and his own talent. The dictates of fashion and taste need affect him only so far as he allows them to. (Financial expediency may make its own demands!) To the student embarking on a textile course, or to the interested layman, it might be worth defining these twin roles.

The commercial designer must develop particular characteristics. He must have some idea of the development and origins of fashion, and an understanding of the market of today which he intends to supply. A commercial design need not necessarily be good to sell well – what the public wants is not always what the designer wants to give it. For a design to sell it must be commercial, and therefore it is up to the designer to produce good, saleable designs which are new or fresh or innovative, yet acceptable to the customer.

Fig. 1.7 Fabrics may be designed flat, but are seldom seen flat.
(a) Design by Jane Nelson

Any visit to a cross-section of fabric stores will immediately reveal both ends of the fabric industry in terms of quality of cloth and design. The most complicated or multicoloured designs are not necessarily the most expensive, and the most interesting or effective designs are often the simplest.

The designer in printed textiles works with, and enjoys the limitations and possibilities inherent in the use of repeat. His textile may be designed flat, but it is seldom seen flat; it may consist of a small or large motif, or basic design, but will ultimately be viewed over a large area, complete with all the rhythms that arise out of repeat. He may refine the use of colour for maximum impact, but the ultimate colour mixing will not be in his hands.

(b) Design by Carole Graham

In the world of fashion textiles the designer faces the most difficult of problems: the forecasting of new trends, which may in many cases be entirely different from designs that fill the previous seasons portfolio. To a greater or lesser degree fashion controls all the designs produced for the commercial market, and the fact that a design might last only one or two seasons is all the more reason for making its short-lived appearance a memorable one! The textile world is a precarious one for the free-lance textile designer.

However, even before considerations of fashion, the student must consider right from the start problems of scale and application. Obviously a small geometric or floral design would be completely lost on a large garment. (In fact this may be the intention.) Many designs are simply to give a background colour or emphasis to the cut of a garment. Conversely, a large-scale pattern or motif would be fragmented on a small garment, and if not actually rendered meaningless, its appearance would certainly be drastically altered.

Stripes may appear to 'zing' or dazzle the eye; motifs may occur in inappropriate places; certain combinations of colours may produce an 'optical grey' at a distance, and directional designs may be too expensive to use in the fashion industry due to cutting and production economy. A large-scale motif may look perfectly acceptable when seen flat, but draped around a figure it could take on new, or even comic suggestions. All these aspects must be taken into account by the fashion textiles designer.

The textile craftsman is ultimately working in another world. Now that commercial production of textiles precludes the use of woodblock or, to some extent, hand-screen printing, and when batik effects can be photographically reproduced via roller or screen prints, the craftsman becomes more an artist, producing one-off articles whose rarity value can make them collectable objects.

Yet the craftsman has been traditionally separate from the artist: the artist as the ideas man who uses the media to express those ideas, and the craftsman, whose ideas often arise from the characteristics of the materials with which he worked.

And herein lies the temptation that awaits us – the media that we use are so seductive that they carry us away! Just look at the smooth translucency of porcelain which does not need any embellishment to bring out its most beautiful characteristics. The patterns made by interwoven rush and cane that were originally developed to fulfil a function are so decorative in their own right that their function can almost seem of secondary importance. It is seldom necessary to gild the lily! (see Fig. 1.8).

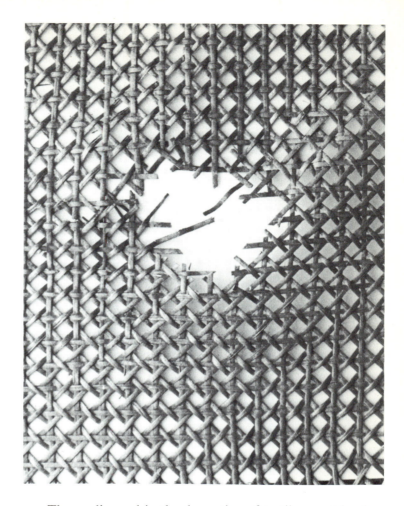

Fig. 1.8 Pattern created by function

The media used in the decoration of textiles must be the most seductive of all. Intense, immediate colour and instant results – which, if not always predictable, usually make an impact of some kind – have long made textile crafts appealing to the amateur. (It is probably due to this aspect of textile crafts that they have taken so long to live down their 'woman's institute' or 'hobby' image.)

The professional craftsman is aware of the traps that await in an area where tradition and cliché are frighteningly close relatives. The limitations that surround the commercial designer are often a blessing in disguise, whereas the lack of limitations that the craftsman enjoys have caused many a downfall!

When given the opportunity, it is just too easy to cram every idea, colour and technique into one piece of work. Carried away by technique, design can often become second best. Sometimes, if lacking in ideas, it is tempting to compensate by virtuoso technique. This is rarely successful – or necessary. Often the most simple *mark* or brush-stroke is enough to please the eye, and the intrinsic beauty of many materials and media is best shown in their simplest form. (Remember the porcelain?) The impact of a simple mark repeated again and again can seldom be improved as a two-dimensional design. Conversely, an over-familiar motif or image can become so trite or visually objectionable that all pleasure in the effects of dye on fabric can be completely overshadowed.

It is only by combination of sensitive design and most suitable technique, used with understanding, that a craft work can be produced that appeals to the senses without offending the aesthetic!

Fortunately, within our art schools students are encouraged to develop personal ideas, and have time to do so. Because of the emphasis placed on good design they are not forced to rely on technique as a compensation, but are able to develop the two aspects of crafts as an integral part of each other. The student is also in the fortunate position of being surrounded by other designers, working in different fields of design.

Textile design has links with all these fields, and no matter which area *you* are working in you cannot afford to be out of touch with the others. You should be aware of all the trends that come and go in art and design, and understand the place of design in art history. There will always be cross-pollination among the arts, and you can exploit this fact to your advantage. By keeping in touch with current and past trends and keeping an open eye, you can produce work that is skilled, exploratory, significant, and above all, decorative and beautiful.

CHAPTER 2

Design sources and resources

The sources of inspiration for design are infinite. Having considered, at some length, the importance of design to the craftsman, we only have to look at the art of the so-called 'primitive' peoples to realise that each one of us is born with an innate sense of design. In most 'civilised' cultures, children soon learn to see the world through the eyes of adults, absorbing considerations of 'taste' and 'realism' that eventually distort their vision. Primitive artists retain a direct and spontaneous reaction to their surroundings. Drawing from instinct and a direct experience of nature, they work untrammelled by the things that affect our complicated life styles. The simplest line or shape grows out of folklore or magic, and abstract design is often a cipher for the real world. Birds and beasts are represented with a child-like directness by these artists, who, delighting so much in the colour and pattern with which they represent their world, experience life at first hand.

These peoples, because of the influx of consumer goods and the development of tourism, have been increasingly exposed to influences and products that they have not encountered before, and which they are utilising in many unusual and exciting ways. Our mundane has become their exotic, just as their everyday experiences are extraordinary and unreal to us. The plastic and tin trappings and wrappings of sophisticated society take on new meaning when recycled and used by people who are unfamiliar with their original use.

With all our conditioned assumptions and prejudices, we can never react completely spontaneously to any situation or object. Nevertheless, we can *learn* to look around us with a fresh eye. Since Andy Warhol introduced us to his celebration of the banal with screen prints of Coca Cola bottles and soup cans, we have opened our eyes to a whole new range of subject-matter. Humorous elements can arise from the juxtaposition of incongruous images, or from unexpected changes in scale and dimension. By keeping an open mind, we can react afresh to things as if they are new each time we see them.

So we have finally been liberated from restrictions and are free to use any media to express our ideas. Since the 1960s, when the use of hallucinogenic drugs and the increasing influence of art-school-educated pop musicians led to the vogue for stunning visual stage effects, we have come to accept media such as lasers and neon as art forms in their own right. Exhibitions of neon sculptures and holograms have since become commonplace. We are familiar with earthworks and wrapped buildings as Art, and have seen sculptures, in the form of piles of bricks and sand in national art galleries Fig. 2.1).

Fig. 2.1 We are no longer shocked by the unexpected in our art galleries ('Equivalent viii' by Carle André.)

So now we are free to impose our own limitations, and to accept or reject those set by the media in which we choose to work. The most stringent limitations are those forced upon us by our own preconceptions, and we must learn to look beyond them, and to redefine them.

The use of materials, for example: glass is brittle, fragile and sharp; water is fluid and mobile; wood is hard; fabric is soft. We see these materials all around us in their most obvious forms, and yet familiarity prevents us determining their true characteristics and the changes that can be brought about to exploit them. We forget the steel-like qualities of toughened industrial glass, or the fluidity of molten glass. We use frozen water when it becomes hard and brittle ice, and handle softwood – pulp – in the shape of newspapers every day. Yet when do we recall their origins? It is never necessary. The familiarity with which we view everyday materials makes us immune to their potential. When we come to use them

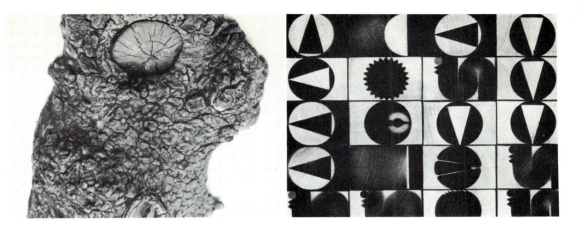

Fig. 2.2 Materials and their uses.
(a) A gnarled piece of wood
(b) Part of a mah-jong set in scorched holly. Designed by Michael Gurney in the furniture school of the Royal College of Art and made by Ron Lenthall

ourselves, we are aware of the many forms they can take, but we often use them in their most obvious shape (Fig. 2.2).

It is fascinating to see the unusual ways in which materials and media have been used over the centuries, and the ways in which they can, superficially, be made to resemble each other (see Fig. 2.3). By using materials inventively it becomes easier to understand their true potential, and to exploit it. The limitations of media and materials are not the only ones that have a bearing on our work. Restrictions can also be imposed by commercial methods of production, finance, or personal taste. It is important not to accept limitations without question; it is the job of the designer to understand, and exploit them, and it can be rewarding to do so. Working to a brief or a set project can develop ideas that might not have surfaced were the designer working within broader outlines. Getting 'much out of little' is challenging and profitable.

So where do printed textiles come into all this? The design of textiles has its own special characteristics which will be explained throughout this book. Textile design can follow several directions, depending on the approach that is chosen. Recently, craft textiles have been taken more seriously as an art form, although commercial design is the area of textiles with which most people are familiar. Pattern on fabrics has always been an important part of our surroundings. As a two-dimensional decorative art, commercial textile design does not have a message to convey (unlike graphic design, for example). Its prime intention has always been apparent in its most obvious form, i.e. the embellishment of surface. This surface 'decoration' (for want of a better word), whether it takes the form of commercial pattern design or fine art on fabric, can be arrived at via various starting-points:

Fig. 2.3 Materials can be made
to resemble each other.
(a) Patchwork quilt
(b) Persian tiles

(c) Screen print
(d) Stained glass

(e) Lace
(f) Wrought iron

1. By the use of drawing from life as a source of ideas for figurative or abstract designs.
2. By the use of pattern and repeat systems based on geometry.
3. By the use of colour as a prime subject in its own right.
4. By the use of print-making media to the exclusion of subject-matter, i.e. by allowing design to develop from the marks made by the tools used.

Geometry will eventually intrude into some forms of textile design because of the need for repeat. 'Drawing' may come into the use of geometry, due to the preconceived associations that we tend to make between the real world and abstract pattern. Colour is the single most important element in textiles as it has such a direct bearing on all aspects of design.

You will probably use many different approaches in your career as a designer, and will not necessarily always work in a particular way, or style.

No matter which approach you employ to make a start, any time spent in galleries and museums will confirm the feeling that 'it has all been done before'. The truth is that it *has* all been done before, but by using a sensitive and exploratory approach it is possible for you to produce something fresh and apparently new, even from the most obvious beginnings.

From time immemorial the same subject-matter has been used and re-used by artists who have adapted it to their own ends. Certain motifs or styles suggest particular eras or cultures, and with experience it becomes easy to recognise them, and even place them chronologically. You may see familiar designs or recurrent themes running through the history of design, but you will notice that each designer has used them in his own way. *Your* task might be the reinterpretation of the most over-exposed motif: Take a flower. How many hundreds of thousands of floral motifs could there be in any one museum? Each one of them is a different interpretation. Even excluding textile design, carpet design, ceramics, architectural decoration, and jewellery, in the area of painting alone, the unending supply of floral images reveals all the different approaches that can be made to one subject.

Look at the way in which the same subject has been treated at different times, and by different artists. Consider the media that they have used, and the results they have achieved (Fig. 2.4). You will see figurative and semi-abstract styles, hard-edged graphic images, and soft, over-blown handling of paint. Try to feel the artists reactions, and the

Fig. 2.4 Look at the way that a subject is treated by different artists.
(a) Flowers in a terracotta vase, by Van Huijsum

responses they have made. One person may have captured a fleeting impression of a flower, another may have made a careful study of it. One may have abstracted it to form part of non-figurative composition, and yet another may have used it as a symbol to signify a situation or feeling.

Each artist has a personal aim when approaching his subject. A botanical illustrator, in showing the detailed structure of a flower in the clearest and least emotional way, makes a scientific record for posterity. A Japanese brush artist

(b) Japanese water-colour, by Sato Suiseki

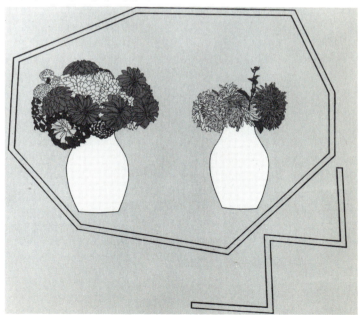

(c) Vases of flowers, by Patrick Caulfield

may come closer to revealing the 'feel' of the flower. By his lightness of touch, and sureness of vision after years of contemplation, he may manage to invoke in his audience reactions and senses other than those of sight alone.

In the light of your understanding of the intentions of other artists and craftsmen, you may see your own experiences from a fresh viewpoint.

The way in which you investigate your subject need not necessarily result in an endless stream of dry, dead drawings and studies in which your interest dwindled long before any worthwhile conclusion was reached. The best way to research a subject is to explore it in many different ways, and with different approaches. By doing this you will continually find new stimuli, and your personal style and method of working will evolve and change along with your developing interests.

Do not, in addition, allow your preconceptions about textile design to dictate the type of subject-matter that you use, or the way in which you treat it. Do not rely on a particular style to make a drawing more elaborate, unless that aspect is to become an intrinsic part of a design. By drawing in a consciously mannered style, you will make your drawing more superficial. Although the *end*-product of textile design may be said to be 'superficial' (i.e. surface) decoration, a more effective result will always be arrived at by sincere investigation. A genuine approach will result in a more personal piece of work, and one that, because it is the result of a unique reaction, should not be a cliché. Of course, style is very important to textile design as it is so closely allied to fashion, and content, in terms of 'meaningful marks' or 'significant statements', does not have much of a place in fashion design. However, although a piece of work may be glossy or glamorous, this does not exclude the need for real sensitivity. A concern for the quality of the marks that you make will lead to a discerning and sympathetic understanding of the use of design and media.

As for subject-matter, today we no longer need feel that we have to turn to the obviously decorative subject as a source of design ideas. It is very easy for the young designer to appreciate the beauty of birds, butterflies, or flowers – all the work has already been done by nature. What is left is an interpretation of something that is already beautiful, and it becomes increasingly difficult to produce work that looks original using such over-exposed imagery.

How much more difficult it is to appreciate or use the more unlikely sources of ideas. Set yourself the challenge of finding the most ugly or unappealing object you can. Spend time drawing it or investigating it in different ways.

Eventually, from its colour, its texture, or the suggestions it makes to you, will arise ideas for a design. Most of the shock effects of exhibiting banal or 'found' objects have passed, but in their place is the acceptance that anything can be called 'Art' or used in the name of art.

Make collections of found objects, or photographs of found objects, even rubbish. (The most attractive and the most repellent objects will always intrude upon your vision, so why limit yourself to only one half of the subject matter that is available to you?) Look at metamorphosis and the process of decay and change. We can all appreciate the fresh beauty of a young unblemished face, but how much more intriguing it is to look at the lined and furrowed surface that is the face of a very old person. There is a sensual pleasure that can easily be had from handling a smoothly sanded and turned piece of wood; rid of its most obvious surface texture it becomes smooth and pristine. Now imagine the pieces of driftwood washed up on the beach, or an old dead tree. Feel their convolutions and time-worn textures, and appreciate the beauty of decay that is all around you.

All the elements change things that come into contact with them. Fire, water, weather (and man!) are constantly ringing the changes in our environment, leaving things unfinished or partially destroyed. There is always talk of 'decaying inner-city areas' with their crumbling brickwork and stark inhumanity. It is not difficult for the artist as an outsider, to see beauty in the pattern and texture of worn brickwork, peeling multilayered wallpapers, and the steel and concrete debris of partially demolished houses (Fig. 2.5). Look in the streets, and all around you you will see the rich patterns produced by the wasting of layers – old lettering on shop-fronts, broken mosaics, torn posters on hoardings, and crumbling paintwork.

In contrast, we are surrounded by the gaudy packaging of the consumer age, bombarded with colour and pattern on all sides – and the delights inside these packages! Multiples of all shapes and sizes. Edible man-made patterns. Pasta, crunchy cat-food, biscuits, popcorn, toffees, and candies. The list is endless, and the shapes intriguing.

Try to draw these objects, treating them as you would a 'serious' still life. Stick them down and take rubbings from them. Ink them and print with them. Paint patterns on them which will distort or camouflage their moulded surfaces. In bypassing the obvious, you will open your eyes to all kinds of new possibilities (see Fig. 2.6). During your work on these objects, comparisons will suggest themselves, recurrent images will occur, and similarities will become apparent. These mass-produced products say all kinds of things about the people that buy them, and the way in which they are made. When using natural forms it is interesting to trace the origins of particular styles in which they are used as motifs. The lack of existing visual information on the more unfamiliar subject-matter – at least, unfamiliar in a particular context –

Fig. 2.5 The strange beauty of decay.
(a) Demolition
(b) Peeling bark
(c) 'Peeling wall', by Ernst Haas

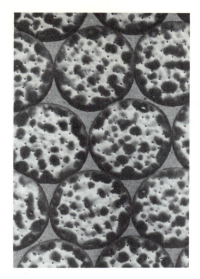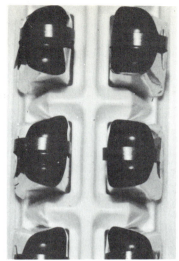

Fig. 2.6   Multiples!
(a) Biscuits
(b) Packaged chocolates
(c) Painted pasta bows

Fig. 2.7   The zany patterns of the
1950s. From the collection of
Alan Flux

encourages you to experience it at first hand. It was this free and spontaneous approach to new and exciting objects that led to the zany designs of the 1950s, when every conceivable surface was covered in a sea of unexpected motifs inspired by a new life style (see Fig. 2.7).

By continually exploring unlikely forms, and storing images, you will gradually free yourself to receive stimulus from many different (and unlikely!) sources, and your scope will be widened.

So many students bemoan the fact that they 'cannot draw'. Perhaps they really are incapable of producing 'photographic' or 'realistic' drawings. Fortunately, all the mechanical methods of reproduction that are at our disposal today can mean that a lack of drawing skills need not be the enormous drawback that it might once have been. After all, the end-product is often intended to be simply an attractive piece of decoration, not necessarily anything more, and it is not 'cheating' to use photographic and reproductive machinery for the purpose for which it is intended!

The important thing is to *observe*. Arm yourself with a camera, and keep it with you wherever you go. Photography can be used in many different ways, not least as the means of building up a valuable reference library. Collect photographs, cuttings, and photocopies of similar and dissimilar things. Compile lists, and make visual comparisons – cobwebs and lace, iron chains and knitting, steel roof structures and giant animal skeletons.

Learn how to collect references, and how to use them. There are libraries in every town, and even if there is not an art gallery or museum near by, postcards are easily come by. Photocopying machines are available to all now in public libraries and offices, and they are a useful means of instantly producing multiples. All these places exist for your benefit. Make use of them! Make your own collections of things that interest you – graphic ephemera, painted or patterned china, old fabrics, toys (Fig. 2.8).

Read the newspapers and journals, and collect articles and reviews of exhibitions. Try to visit as many exhibitions as you can, keeping in touch with artists working in all the different fields, and collect reproductions of their work. Use the experiences of other artists and cultures to suggest ways in which you could enrich your own work. If you want to use a particular motif or idea, look around and discover how it has been used before.

Surround yourself with stimuli: keep your own scrapbooks, and have a changing display of visuals on your pin-board, or in your working area.

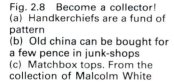

Fig. 2.8   Become a collector!
(a) Handkerchiefs are a fund of pattern
(b) Old china can be bought for a few pence in junk-shops
(c) Matchbox tops. From the collection of Malcolm White

Explore media for yourself, and see how other artists have used the media that *you* use.

Always try to experience things directly. Most children have taken rubbings from coins and raised patterned surfaces, and you will find that rubbings can provide the best representation of a textured surface. (The use of rubbings in printing can also produce surprising results.) There are textured surfaces in every house and street, and often the most interesting ones are those where time and wear have worn away the edges, and fractured the surface into further unintentional patterns. Colour your rubbings; combine them, or work on a coloured or patterned ground. By overlaying patterns or building them up on a background, you can reverse the peeling process, adding on instead of taking away.

When starting to draw, use the basic approach – you may learn from it. Make a simple line using different media – a pen line, a charcoal line, a painted line, a smeared line, a raised line, an engraved line. A very fine line on a large scale may look weak, invisible, or meandering (indeed this may be the intention!), when done with a large paintbrush the same line can appear dynamic and powerful.

Try to stretch the media, making them do things that do not come naturally to them – large, very fine pen drawings, and small drawings done with a large brush. Try to suggest mass and tone with a pen, and with a pencil, and see the different results – the smooth flow of a graded pencil tone, and the cross-hatching or massed dots of pen-work.

Use and investigate materials that do not immediately appeal to you, and ask yourself why they do not appeal. Do not worry if you cannot handle them at first – you do not have to achieve success every time! And do not worry about what your results look like – after all a pen line is permanent, and what matter that it cannot be rubbed out? The searching line has its own beauty when repeated over and over again in an attempt to find just the right expression. The very spontaneity of water-colour can liberate the tightest drawing style, and the softness of charcoal or pastel can soften the most insensitive line.

You will eventually find the medium that suits your intentions and the scale in which you are working (these may change with each new project) and, by experimenting, can help free your work from constraints (Fig. 2.9).

When working with mass and tone, look around you at shapes that create mass. When working in line, look at things that, are by nature, linear. Collect photographs of railings, railway lines, fences, girders, branches, and grasses (Fig. 2.10). Make drawings of lines formed by the repetition of elements – beads, strings of lights, trees on the horizon. Observe how grids are formed by lines that cross. Look at grids that form supports, and how their structure seems to be fragmented by the shapes or forms they support.

Fig. 2.9 Certain media will suit certain projects. Be versatile!
(a) Photocopied magazine collage, by Sheila Schmidt

Fig. 2.9   Certain media will suit
certain projects. Be versatile!
(b)   Paper and plastic collage, by
Kerry Tuckett

Fig. 2.10   Collect references that
relate to the project in hand: line
and tone

Play with various surfaces. Gather a quantity of different papers and cloths together. Cut them, stretch them, fold them, score them, etch them, bond them together, stitch them, distort them, burn them. Their surfaces will suggest ways in which they can be used – shiny cover papers, handmade Japanese papers, fine tissue papers, newsprint, board, and blotting-papers. Try to make a mark with a certain medium on a particular paper or surface, then try it on all the other surfaces you have available. Be methodical; try each medium on every surface, and without drawing at all you will discover hundreds of design possibilities. The simple combination of texture and colour can be so strong that no other element is called for.

Should the use of colour zerox be available to you, you will have the opportunity to distort the colour – and to some extent the form – of your design. Given control over the colour you can produce strange and exciting results, creating images and effects that are a long way from your original. By using the right type of paper, you can even produce colour zerox prints on cloth by heat transfer.

As the use of colour zerox becomes more widespread, its full potential is being realised. It can be used as a record, as a quick method of producing coloured multiples, and as an art form in its own right. Colour zerox produces its own peculiar colour-separation effects that can be varied at the turn of a switch, and these instant results can be great fun to play with.

Colour zerox can produce fascinating effects by distortion, and distortion can be used in many different ways to give you ideas for design. Distortion is an important element in textile design, as few designs are seen flat, and all are changed by the way in which they are hung.

You will see distortion all around you, in many shapes and forms (Fig. 2.11). Look at the images created by distortion – the way things appear when seen through figured or reeded glass, and the overlay of images that is formed by reflections in a window that resemble a multi-exposure photograph. Draw the world reflected in broken or shattered glass – flawed, or curved glass, baubles, mirror foil, bull's-eye windows, and mirror mosaics. Fragmentation occurs in many ways that can give you ideas for design. Holes are made in some surfaces, through which other things are seen – slatted blinds, or net and lace curtains. The image is broken up, but still forms a whole.

The distortion formed by light playing on uneven surfaces can form strange surreal patterns. Look at the effects of sunlight, and the type of shadows it creates. Make drawings in the sun at different times of day, and throughout the seasons.

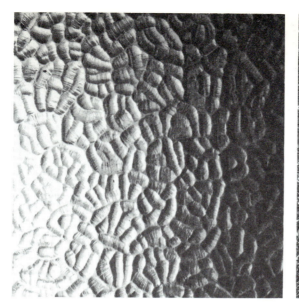

Fig. 2.11 Distortion.
(a) Figured glass
(b) Ruched fabric

You will see the crisp sharpness of sunlight on snow, and the strong autumn sun fragmenting leaves and trees as it shines through them.

If you are lucky enough to live near a swimming-pool with a steel and glass roof you will discover the most beautiful patterns reflected in the water. Get permission to go to the poolside before the pool is open. Look at the tiles as they go down under the water, and how the reflections of the windows and the steel-strutted roof are almost, but not quite, straight. And then, as the first swimmers arrive, the gradual disturbance of the water that takes place. The reflections fragment and break; they float on the top of the waves and ripples. Dark patches appear, moving with the light; little areas of pattern, trailing through the water. Capture the ripples sent out to the edge of the pool by the first person who disturbs its surface. Try to draw these effects on the spot, or at least photograph them, experiencing them at first hand (Fig. 2.12).

Make your own distorting surfaces by wrapping regularly patterned papers around three-dimensional objects. See how stripes curve, and spots elongate. The effects might give you some ideas as to the changes that will be brought about in your designs by draping and hanging.

And finally, having investigated all the 'intellectual' routes through drawing and analysis, enjoy the results of chance, and

Fig. 2.12   Pattern distorted on water

Fig. 2.13   'Action Painting' after the style of Jackson Pollock

produce random designs. Look at the work of artists who use chance to influence their work (see Fig. 2.13). Experience for yourself the fun that can be had playing with chance. Cut paper, and glue it where it falls, make blottings from inked surfaces, splash paint, and allow chance to form your designs. And so, those of you inhibited by a lack of drawing skills can learn to abstract from a source, to observe in your own way, and to respond personally to your environment. Eventually, by exploitation of your media, and a sensitivity of approach, you may be able to produce beautiful designs without recourse to the more obvious approaches or subject matter.

Compile your own visual and written references of design sources and resources. The following list may help you make a start.

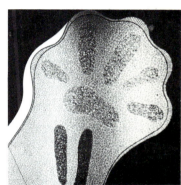

Fig. 2.14 Museums, galleries, and popular culture

Museums; art galleries; pop culture (Fig. 2.14)

Persian and Indian miniatures
Microphotography
Graphics and advertising
Typography
'Street art'
Theatre and cinema
Travel
Art nouveau and art deco
Saxon carvings
Greek painting
Tapestries
Clocks and their mechanisms
Modern art exhibitions
Juke-boxes
Illustration and illustrators
Collage

Chinese paper cuts
Surrealism
Painting
Sculpture
Ceramics
Print-making
Maps
Television
Amusement arcades
Kitch
Stained glass
Wrought iron
Pop culture
Computer games
Neon

'Dada'
Architectural details
Fashion design, past and present
Celtic forms
Egyptian painting
Persian and oriental carpets
Shadow puppets and dolls
Mosaics
Colour and black and white zerox
Mobiles
Nostalgia
Photography
Toys
African, Javanese, and Japanese textiles
Paintings
Collections of ephemera

Organic forms (Fig. 2.15)

Plants, leaves, and grasses
Trees
Flowers and plants
Fruit and vegetables
Camouflage
Feathers
Snowflakes
Entomology

Geology
Cytology
Fur
Fish scales
Precious stones
Water
Wood grain
Butterflies

Photomicrography
Fire
Marble
Skins and animal coverings
Shells – sea shells and animal shells
Skeletons
Malacology

Fig. 2.15   Organic forms

Inorganic forms (Fig. 2.16)

Science museums   Machines   Steel and glass structures
Motor vehicles   Motors   Wrought iron
Balloons and kites   Cogs and wheels   Tracery on architecture
Construction and demolition   Computers   Bicycles
Molecular structure   Clocks   Aeroplanes, rockets, and their markings
Brick and stone   Engines
Mechanisms   Circuit boards

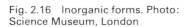

Fig. 2.16   Inorganic forms. Photo: Science Museum, London

CHAPTER 3

Pattern

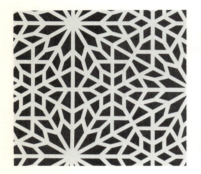

Fig. 3.1 The faces of pattern.
Pattern dictated by existing
shapes.
(a) Islamic geometric pattern
(b) Floral tiles
(c) Marble mosaic path

All textiles consist of pattern. We may have to look closely to see it, but it is there, visible, in the structure of the cloth. The very act of passing one thread over another creates weaves such as herringbone, check, and twill, that are part of the structure of the fabric and which create a more-than-surface pattern.

The textile print designer is a 'painter of fabrics' whose job it is to apply on to its surface a pattern that does not necessarily relate to the weave of a cloth. It is this surface texture, already created by someone else, that can most surely influence the design used upon it. The density of the cloth, its weight, and its appearance, are all factors that must be constantly borne in mind when designing for fabrics.

Unlike the painter, the designer must envisage his fabric being used (and not just viewed) in many different ways, and must acknowledge very early on the effects on colour and pattern of folding and draping.

It is in the field of pattern design that most textile designers work, and, as designers, we realise very early on that pattern is all around us. In our surroundings we constantly see the blending of the practical and the ornamental that results in conscious and incidental pattern.

Fig. 3.2 Pattern: structure and embellishment

Look at old buildings; their solid construction topped with decorative friezes. One pattern arises from structure, the other from a desire for embellishment which, as such, has no other function than that of decoration (Fig. 3.2).

When dealing with textile design the terms 'pattern' and 'design' become difficult to separate. 'Design' is generally accepted as meaning anything that is *designed* for a specific purpose. Man-made patterns are designed – their purpose is to be decorative – but design does not always incorporate pattern. Dictionary definitions can sometimes be interesting: the designer working in areas other than textile design often uses pattern as 'a model to be copied'. The textile designer, on the other hand, uses pattern in another form – as 'an artistic arrangement of repeating or corresponding parts'.

PATTERN AND REPEAT

It is the 'arrangement of repeating or corresponding parts' that defines pattern as *we* know it. Pattern and design do have elements in common, but the one characteristic of pattern that separates it totally from design is the repeat. The creation of pattern is dependent upon repetition. A non-repeating pattern is a design, or a motif. A motif is a complete entity; repeat it, and it becomes a series of motifs; it rarely incorporates the elements that will constitute pattern. The motifs, or shapes, being identical, will bear relation to each other, but, as they are self-contained, will almost certainly lack the characteristics necessary to create the rhythm that occurs when a shape has been designed with repeat in mind. Subtle and exciting (and even sometimes, undesirable) rhythms and forms can occur when a shape that is designed specifically for repeat, is put into repeat.

In pattern design the original shape (or series of shapes within a unit) can be repeated in many different ways, the original unit being seen simply as part of a larger whole.

Tile patterns are the most obvious means of illustrating this principle. Tiles, by necessity, are small identical units that align with each other to cover an area which is larger than themselves. The outline edges of the tiles form a variety of geometric grids, depending on the shape of the tile. The shapes within the tile, which are also repeated, create new focal points when those which touch the edges or corners of the tile are aligned with an identical shape on another tile (Fig. 3.3).

Fig. 3.3 Tile patterns: shapes contained in small units form spreading patterns when aligned with other identical units

The term 'tile pattern' has, in textiles, come to mean a rigid geometric unit that repeats like a tile. It contains shapes that do not protude from it, but form a spreading continuous pattern when the 'tile' is repeated. The outline of the tile is often visible, and sometimes forms an integral part of the design.

It may be said that the tile format is always used in one form or another in textile design, as every repeating design is governed by simple geometric guidelines, and the most free design repeats along the same lines as the most geometric.

After expending so much effort in the pursuit of a personal approach to design it may seem basic or impersonal to consider these geometric foundations of pattern. However, even the most sensitive and personal piece of work must eventually rely on geometry if it is to be printed in repeat.

Fortunately, these geometric 'guidelines' are not always visible eventually, neither should one be hampered by the need to use them. A geometric outline such as a simple square or rectangle can be placed around a completely irregular shape or set of shapes which are already in existence, and ignored until it is needed. The guidelines are the means by which the shapes are accurately placed at each repeat. The shapes within the guidelines are adjusted to fit together like a jigsaw, and the guidelines are eventually removed.

The clue to success when working with repeats is to familiarise yourself with the various methods of repeating a design, and how each method can affect a design by shifting emphases and focal points (see Figs. 3.14 and 3.17). Once the types of repeat are understood (and it is fun experimenting with them, not hard work!) it becomes easier to create a design with the potential of repeat in mind.

Pattern is infinite, and a well-designed pattern always gains from repetition.

This term 'repeat', when used in textile design, can mean several different things. At its most obvious, the repeat is the means of increasing the coverage of a small design. This aspect of repeat is obviously of vital importance in the production of commercial printed textiles where the repeat not only adds a sense of harmony to the final effect, but is usually the only way in which the design can be mechanically reproduced on cloth. 'The repeat' is also used to multiply a large design that already covers the width of a cloth, so that it repeats, without visible joins, along the length of the cloth (see Fig. 3.20). The other type of printed textile, 'the painting' or one-off hanging, employs repeat in a more subtle way – if at all.

In your drawings you will have found that rhythm is a very important element. Without it a drawing appears static and lifeless. A sense of rhythm is often brought about by a suggestion of repeat. It may be the repetition of a certain type of shape, or simply a particular subdivision of space. Repetition, even in its most subtle form, can lend a sense of harmony and order to a design (Fig. 3.4).

When working with pattern, rhythm is of vital importance. The original design contains all the elements necessary to create a repeating rhythm. If the design is very static it will form a rigid pattern in repeat. If it is more fluid, containing diagonal or flowing lines, a more rhythmic repeat will result, as shapes are formed and directions occur that were not apparent during the early stages.

When a small design is repeated, the edges of that design become particularly important. In a painting, shapes that touch the edge of the canvas end there. It may be *suggested* that they continue into space, but to all practical intents and purposes they finish where the canvas does.

With a textile design all the shapes that touch the edges of the design are powerful features in their own right, as when the design is repeated they can shift its entire emphasis. In repeat they may form disjointed or clashing areas, mirror images, or new focal points. The edges of the design, therefore, must be considered very carefully – they can become its new centre (see Fig. 3.3).

Fig. 3.4 Repetition is the basis of pattern

BASIC GEOMETRIC NETWORKS THAT FORM PATTERN

These are uniformly shaped polygons that can be repeated *ad infinitum* (Fig. 3.5). They can be used: (1) as 'tiles', in which case their outlines form the design itself, or an integral part of it; (2) as sets of guidelines to contain designs which are to be put into repeat; or (3) as guidelines for accurate geometric

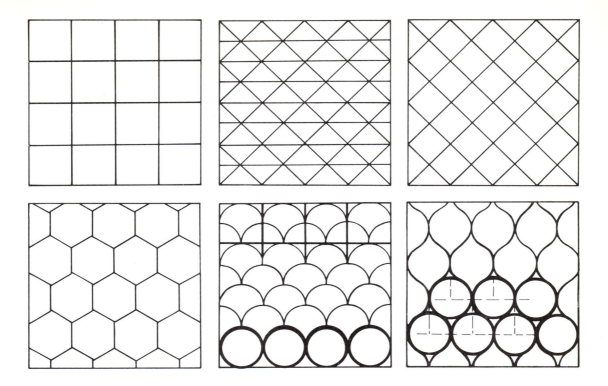

Fig. 3.5 The grid networks that form spreading infinite patern

designs that may involve the use of other networks.

The basic geometric shapes that form the networks on which pattern is based are shown in Fig. 3.5 and are as follows: *The square; The triangle; The diamond; The hexagon; The scale; The ogee.* They are all around you! (see Fig. 3.6)

All these shapes, provided that they are equilateral, can be placed to repeat infinitely. They can contain other (not necessarily geometric) shapes, and the forms taken by *these* shapes in repeat will be dictated by the geometric framework that encloses them.

Most of these easily repeated units are developed from each other, and relate to the square or the circle:

The square evolves from straight lines that cross each other at right angles.

Triangles are formed when rectangles or squares are bisected from one corner to another. They can be arranged to form rectangles, squares, zigzags, and hexagons.

Diamonds occur where groups of squares are diagonally bisected in both directions.

The hexagon is formed from a series of triangles.

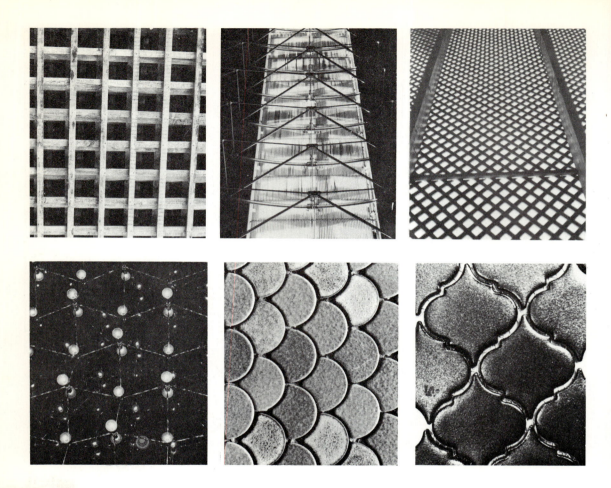

Fig. 3.6 The basic patterns are all around us.
The square
The triangle
The diamond
The hexagon
The scale
The ogee

The circle is a unit which, in itself, cannot be repeated to interlock, although the *ogee* and the *scale* are forms developed from the circle that are repeatable.

The ogee and the scale are built on a network of circles and straight lines; circles laid out on a brick network (see Fig. 3.5) create a series of ogees and scales that are formed from tangential and overlapping circles.

The ogee is a very graceful form much liked traditionally by textile designers (Fig. 3.7).

The scale is a very versatile unit to repeat. If all its vertical and horizontal dimensions are equal it can be repeated in many different ways, turning it about to produce irregular-looking repeats, undulating lines, and 'layered' designs (Fig. 3.8).

Fig. 3.7 Ogee designs

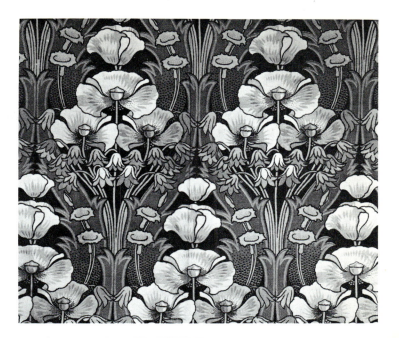

Fig. 3.8 The versatile scale

BASIC METHODS OF REPEAT

Using basic geometry, an enormous number of patterns can be produced. These patterns do not spring from our own personal experience or observation of nature; they involve a different approach; they are pattern-making at its most pure. To the 'painter' of fabrics, intent on developing a highly personal or idiosyncratic viewpoint, they may be of little more concern than to merit merely a passing nod. Even the textile designer may find that only the basic methods of repeat are of interest.

However, one difference between the painter and the commercial designer is that the designer is subject to the whims of fashion. These fashion changes – this year floral, next year geometric – mean that it is in the interest of the designer to take time to explore the potential of geometric pattern. At the very least, as even the most 'free' design relies on geometry to repeat, it is well to understand the basic ways of repeating a design.

The network that we most commonly use today as a series of guidelines for repeat is the square, sometimes altered to

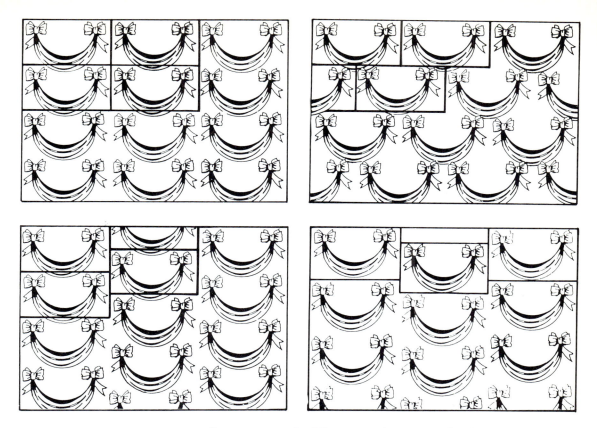

Fig. 3.9 The basic repeat
systems.
(a) The block   (b) The brick
(c) The drop   (d) The step

form a rectangle. The square is so versatile that scores of
geometric designs can be created from it, including chequers,
interlocking bands, zigzags, chevrons, and complex interwoven
forms. The square (or rectangle) by itself, even as a simple
one-level grid, can be repeated in many different ways: it can
be laid out regularly, with each square facing the same way, it
can be mirrored, rotated, 'dropped' alongside another square,
or misplaced to form a brick layout.

The basic methods used to repeat the square (or rectangle)
are as follows (see Fig. 3.9): *The block; The brick; The
drop; The step.*

The block repeat

This is the most simple repeat. The block can be rotated or
mirrored, (flipped over) but its outlines must always be kept
in line (Fig. 3.10(c) and (b)). The most basic block repeat is one

where the block containing a design is positioned so that the design faces the same way at each repeat. The most complex designs can be produced by rotating a block containing geometric patterns. If these are calculated carefully, designs can result in which the outlines of the basic block are totally disguised by the seemingly complicated all-over design.

Look around you at the ways in which the block is used in everyday life. Collect photographs and drawings. What you see may give you ideas for designs, as well as explaining the ways in which basic units are repeated (Figs. 3.10(a)).

Fig. 3.10 The repetition of the basic block.
(a) Block repeat design, by Julie Speechley, in which alternate rows of blocks have been rotated (turned round)

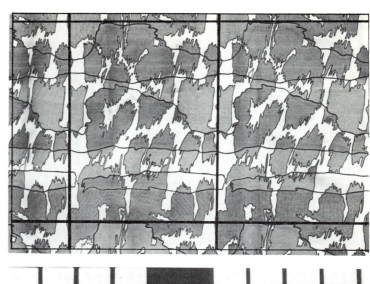

(b) Basic block repeat design, by Belinda Blackwell: 'Skin'

(c) Glass wall

The brick repeat

We are all familiar with the brick as the basic building unit, (Fig. 3.11) and the vast amount of patterned domestic tiles now available means that even the layman has become aware of the ways in which this layout can affect pattern.

In two-dimensional pattern the brick repeat is very useful as it can affect the pattern in several different ways: it gives a design a horizontal and diagonal emphasis; if the outlines of the brick are visible in the design it can give the design a

(b) Fabric print, by Raoul Dufy

Fig. 3.12 Brick repeat in which alternate rows of bricks have been mirrored (note the horizontal emphasis)

sense of solidity and stability; or if the bricks are turned or rotated and their outlines disguised a more unexpected design will result (see Fig. 3.12).

The drop repeat

The drop repeat is a close relative of the brick repeat, in that one rotated 90° creates the other. The main difference between them is that the drop forms a vertical emphasis, and the brick a horizontal one (see Fig. 3.13). The 'drop' repeat is so called because each unit is dropped half-way (or a quarter, or a third) down another unit.

Fig. 3.13   The vertical and
diagonal emphasis of the drop
repeat

The step repeat

The step repeat should not be confused with the drop repeat, although the effects of a *half* drop and a *half* step are the same.

The differences become more apparent when drops and steps other than one-half are used. In a drop repeat, each successive unit drops, and always by the same amount. In drops other than a half, this forms a slanting, or diagonal, emphasis (see Fig. 3.14).

Fig. 3.14
(a) A (one-third) drop creates a diagonal emphasis, and an overall design which is deeper than a step repeat
(b) A step repeat creates a horizontal emphasis, and a shallower design

The step repeat is so called because the tops of the units step up and down. On a step other than a half, this can make a considerable difference to the design in terms of overall size and emphasis (see Fig. 3.14). It is important to recognise the differences between these two types of repeat.

It also should be borne in mind, in the case of all these repeat networks, that the grids formed by the units serve as sets of guidelines only. Unlike the more interesting polygons such as the diamond or scale, these basic rectangle repeats are

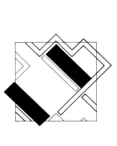

Fig. 3.15 Complex patterns arise when designs that exceed their guidelines are put into repeat.
(a) The original block
(b) The final design

usually used only to position the design, and their outlines are removed once this purpose has been achieved.

As these networks are guidelines only, they should be treated as such, and placed around designs which exceed their edges at some points. This will ensure that eventually they can be removed and not leave noticeable repetitive gaps in the overall design. The rhythms and directional shapes that arise from the repeat cannot do so if the original design is placed within a square or rectangle like a motif, and an interesting pattern will only arise if shapes are allowed to overlap or interlock on the repeat. They can only do this if they exceed their guidelines (see Fig. 3.15).

One way to ensure that the design does repeat in an interesting way is to create the design first (bearing in mind the relevant measurements) and *then* enclose it in a set of geometric guidelines (usually a square or a rectangle). The design can exceed the guidelines at one point, and be enclosed within it at another.

When the guidelines are fitted together in repeat some shapes may clash or overlap – but no obvious guidelines will be visible. Clashing shapes can then be altered to fit, and awkward gaps can be filled in. Gauging the placing of shapes by eye will come with experience.

TESTING, OR 'PROVING' A DESIGN TO JUDGE THE SHAPES IT WILL CREATE IN REPEAT

To see the overall pattern a small design will create when repeated it is necessary to reproduce it several times (this is where the block repeats, etc. come in). By doing this, all the edges and points at which the design repeats with itself can be altered to fit exactly, and unwanted gaps can be filled in.

To test the repeat, the original unit is surrounded by other identical units so that each edge and corner can be checked where it touches another. In practice it is often sufficient to use *one* unit, and surround it only with the relevant edges of the other units that line up with it. If the design is eventually to be printed it can easily be increased in size to fit the screen, by adding more units.

The process used to check the repeat is called 'halving'. In the case of a small design, parts of the design are traced and rubbed down in position, and in the case of a large design, the design is actually cut in half and replaced to form the repeat (Fig. 3.21).

Proving a small design by tracing

The example shown is a block repeat. The same process is used with all repeats.

Procedure

1. Fix the design to a flat surface with tape. Draw a set of *accurate* guidelines around the design to form a square or rectangle.

   It is preferable, at this stage, to have mapped out the main outlines and shapes of the design in pencil. Colour should not be added in great amounts as alterations will undoubtedly have to be made later.

2. Fix a large piece of good-quality tracing paper centrally over the design and take an accurate tracing (any intricate details need not be included). *Include the guidelines* (see Fig. 3.16(a)).

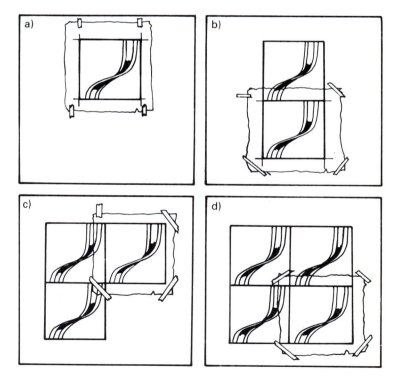

Fig. 3.16 'Proving' a small design to see how it looks in repeat

3. Remove the tracing paper, and draw over the design on the back with a soft pencil, enabling it to be drawn down again the right way up.

4. Take the tracing, and position it beneath the original design, so that the top guideline of the tracing rests against the bottom guideline of the drawing. Ensure that the vertical guidelines are in line. If the guidelines do not line up, this indicates that the original rectangle has not been drawn correctly.
5. Draw the design through, including the guidelines (Fig. 3.16(b)).
6. Now repeat this procedure at the right-hand side of the design, keeping the tracing the correct way up (Fig. 3.16(c)).
7. Remove the tracing again, and position it in the remaining corner. Trace the design through (Fig. 3.16(d)).
8. If the way in which the design repeats is not clear to you, trace down more units around the original.

When the design has been drawn down in this way, you will undoubtedly find that there are disjointed areas at the points of repeat where some shapes do not meet as they should. Shapes may end at one point and not continue, or discordant shapes may clash at a join line.

It may be necessary to reposition some shapes or to adjust or abandon them altogether.

The design can be altered to fit in the following way:

1. Make any necessary adjustments to the original unit in the block of four, extending shapes into other units, or altering them as required.
2. Add all the adjustments accurately to the tracing.
3. Fix the tracing down over each unit in turn, and, by a process of rubbing out and retracing, add all the alterations to each unit.
4. Remove all guidelines except those that form the outside edges of the completed design.

The method of reproducing the design in repeat is the same no matter which type of repeat is used; only the positioning of the tracing is different.

In the case of a mirror repeat, the tracing is used face up/face down to form the mirror image (see Fig. 3.17(a)). It will be necessary to draw the design down in full in several positions to determine the form that the mirror image will take, as the design can be mirrored side to side, as well as top to bottom.

By methodical positioning of the tracing a small unit can be used to produce a wide variety of designs (see Fig. 3.17).

Fig. 3.17 A small simple motif
used to form a variety of designs
using basic repeat systems

When repeating small units, it might become apparent that
certain designs would be more interesting if the units were

a)

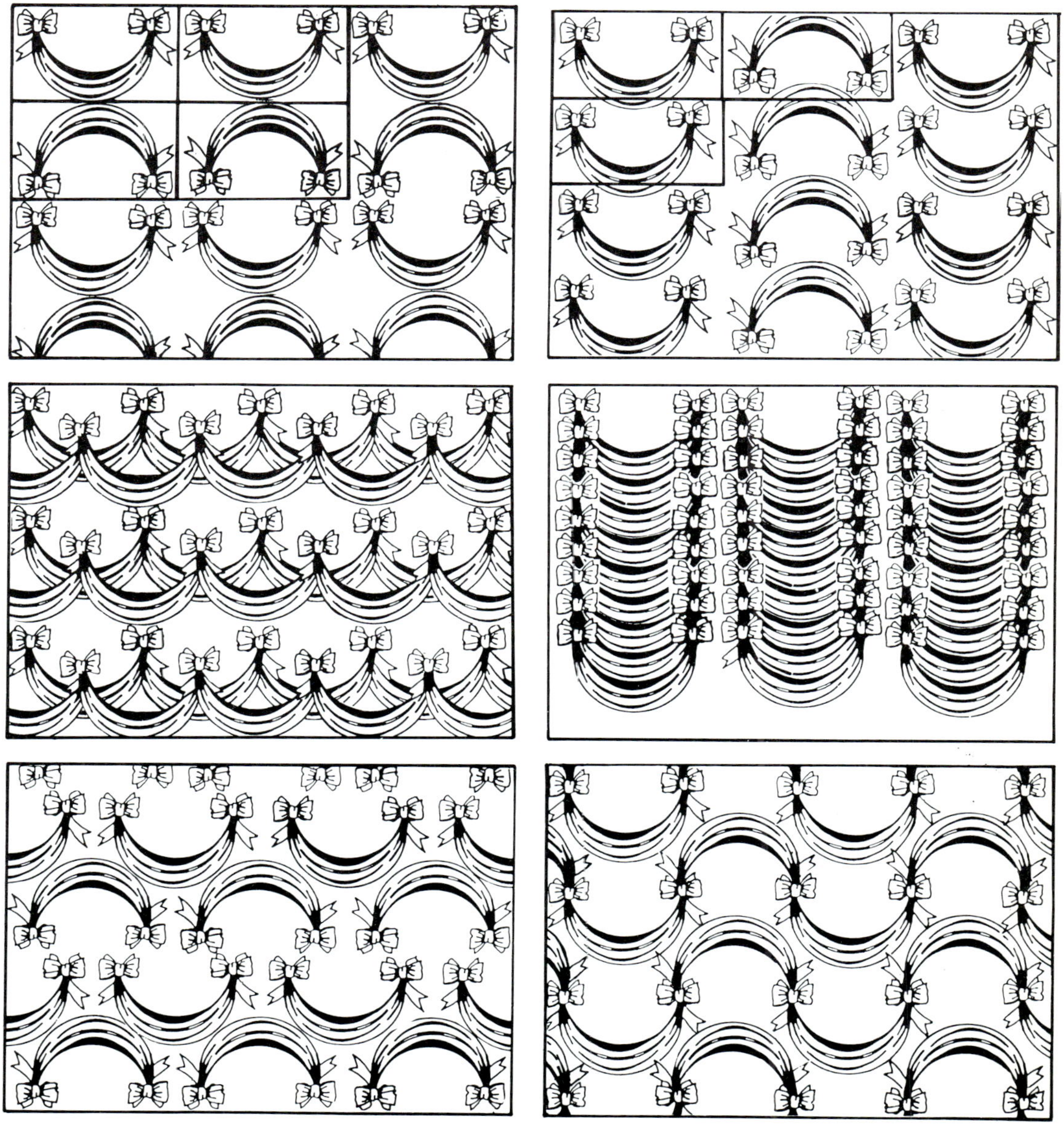

overlapped, or spaced apart (distanced). By overlapping, the size of the rectangle that forms the guidelines is decreased. By distancing units from each other the dimensions of the guidelines are increased (see Figs. 3.18 and 3.19). This fact must be understood, and measurements calculated carefully when designing for specific widths of cloth where the design is expected to repeat at the selvage.

Overlapping – procedure
1. Take an accurate tracing of the original design (Fig. 3.18(a)).

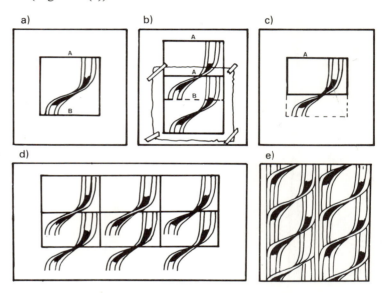

Fig. 3.18 Overlapping the design to close up the repeat

2. Remove the tracing, and place it below the design as before. Now move it over the design until the design overlaps as required, *keeping the guidelines in line* (Fig. 3.18(b)).
   Note that the top line on the tracing (A) has overlapped over the bottom line of the original unit (B). Ensure that the distance of the overlap is equal by measuring it at either side.
3. Transfer the top line on the tracing to its new position on the original design (prick its position through with a pin). This will serve as the new bottom edge to the design. Rub out the original bottom line on the design. (Fig. 3.18(c)).
4. Lay the tracing in its original position over the design, and transfer the altered guideline from the design to the tracing.

This creates a new set of guidelines from which the design protrudes (see Fig. 3.18(c)).

The units can now be fitted together using the guidelines, with parts of the design protruding from one unit into another, and the distance of overlap will not have to be judged by eye (Fig. 3.18(d)).

Distancing to create a more open design

The same basic procedure as used for overlapping is followed to distance the units, leaving spaces in between if needed.

Instead of lapping the tracing over the design, it is distanced from it. The guidelines, as usual, must be kept in line (a precision grid should be used if possible). The new guidelines are added to the tracing and the design in the same way that they are for overlapping, and create a larger, rather than a smaller rectangle (see Fig. 3.19).

Overlapping or distancing can be used with all the types of repeat, and experiment along these lines will show the forms, and dimensions that will result.

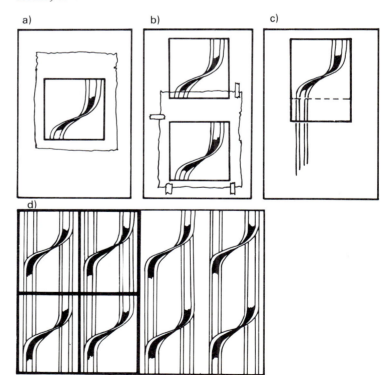

Fig. 3.19 Distancing the design to open it up.
(a) The original design and tracing
(b) The tracing distanced from the design
(c) The guidelines and the design are extended
(d) The final design is more open

Any design that is to be drawn up in repeat must be drawn with the greatest accuracy. Many colleges use precision grids for this purpose. The precision grid normally takes the form of an engraved light box or a thick acetate sheet printed with an accurate square (millimetre) grid. The plastic grid can be used under tracing paper, or under thicker paper if used on a light box.

Graph paper – transparent if possible – is an obvious choice for repeating a design, and where a precision grid is not available it can be used, but *only for the most freely fitting designs*, as graph paper is not sufficiently accurate for close repeats. (The design is drawn directly on to the graph paper in this instance.)

As even the thickness of a pencil lead can distort measurements, only the sharpest, hard pencils should be used when drawing the guidelines for repeats.

'FULL-WIDTH DESIGNS'

A precision grid is of particular use when a design is produced in which the full width of the cloth is used as the measurement of a single unit. A design on this scale is usually used for furnishing fabrics, the design repeating at the selvage, and forming a giant block repeat when widths of fabric are joined together (Fig. 3.20).

This type of design is repeated along the same lines as a smaller design, except that it is normally cut to repeat, instead of being traced. The design may employ as intricate a join as a smaller design, and therefore the cutting of one is as important as the tracing of the other.

Fig. 3.20 A full-width design: 'Olympic symbols', by Liz Picton

56

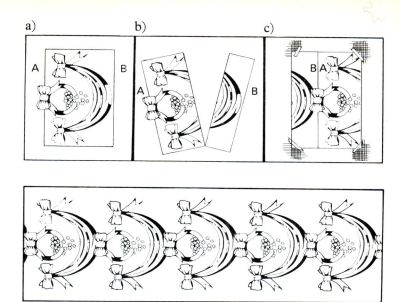

a)   b)   c)

Fig. 3.21   Halving a large design
by cutting, to put it into repeat

Halving large designs to test the repeat

Cutting procedure

Note: If the design is being cut to repeat for *printing*, please refer to Chapter 5 (p. 102) for the cutting procedure. For design on paper only, the following procedure can be used:

1. Enclose the design within an accurate rectangle. The design can protrude from the long sides of it, the rectangle, as usual being simply a set of guidelines (Fig. 3.21(a)).
2. Cut through the design from top to bottom (Fig. 3.21(b)).
3. Tape the left-hand side of the design firmly to a precision grid. (The design could actually have been drawn on to graph paper if a very loose-fitting repeat is being used, and the grid lines on the graph paper used for registration.)
4. Take the right-hand half of the design and place it to the left of the left-hand half, so that edge B rests against edge A, and all vertical and horizontal guidelines are in alignment, both with each other, and with the grid (Fig. 3.21(c)).

    The design can be overlapped at the join between A and B or distanced slightly if required. The guidelines, however, must remain parallel.

At this stage any part of the design can be altered in any way, with one notable exception: any part of the design that touches one or other of the new outside edges must not be changed. As these parts of the design have been cut from each other, any alterations made to them would mean that they would not fit together again in repeat.

A design that covers the full width of the cloth has certain advantages. It enables the designer to work freely over a large area using both large and small shapes; the design can be asymmetric, and its very size ensures impact. Extremely powerful designs can be produced in this way.

One obvious aspect of the full-width design is that neither the brick nor the half-drop repeat can be used. Bearing in mind the diagonal emphasis that can be formed using these systems, such emphasis must be created freely within the large area in the early stages (see Fig. 3.22).

Fig. 3.22 'Billiards', by Liz Picton
A full-width design with diagonal emphases

The strong continuous directional lines of a full-width repeat suggest a certain stability resulting from the construction of the design which is built like a set of large blocks, one beneath the other. Unwanted repeat marks, when they do occur, make their presence felt so powerfully that they can actually become dominant positive features, whereas in a small design they would simply be a recurrent irritant.

Unwanted repeat marks may occur from time to time on all repeats. They may take the form of stripes, or oddly shaped gaps which can seem more eye-catching than the deliberate features of the design. As such, they can obviously be detrimental. One solution to this problem is to try to work out in advance where negative shapes are likely to occur. To help, at the early stage it is useful to keep two unframed mirrors to hand. These can be placed upright at right angles next to each other around two sides of the design, which can then be seen reflected in them in repeat.

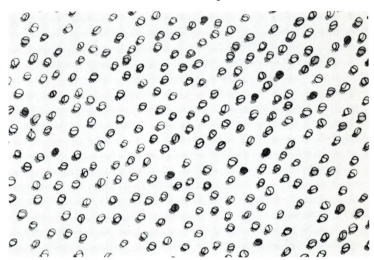

Fig. 3.23 'Tennis balls', a random scatter design by Liz Picton

SMALL 'SCATTERED' DESIGNS

It might seem that a small scattered design is the easiest to produce – simply scatter the 'spots' at random, and allow them to form their own free distribution in repeat. However, the very nature of this type of repeat makes it a prey to unwanted repeat marks. Although the design may look well thought out in the early stages, when it is put into repeat the picture may be an altogether different one! Gaps may occur that were not visible at first, or several small shapes may cluster together at the repeat join. Admittedly, these can be altered when the design is put into repeat on paper, but the more disconcerting mistakes will not be visible until the design is repeated many times on fabric. This is because certain features do not become noticeable or visually irritating until they are picked up by the eye again and again.

If, on the other hand, small shapes are distributed within a small unit which is then itself arranged over a larger area, any unwanted features can be altered easily at the beginning.

Weavers come up against this problem all the time, working as they do with tiny threads, each of which forms a small 'spot' where it appears at the front of the cloth, and they have devised the following system to plan exactly where each small feature will occur and recur, and what its effects will be. At least in this way the stripes, diagonals, clusters, and gaps that appear will be deliberate!

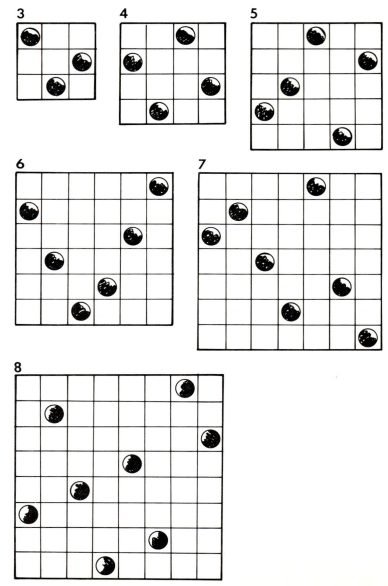

Fig. 3.24 'Placing small shapes to determine how and where they will recur

The regular placement of small motifs

1. Draw a square, and divide it into 3, 4, 5, 6, 7, or 8 small squares in either direction (see Fig. 3.24).
2. Distribute the small motif that is to be scattered, in this particular way: in the 3-square unit (three in either direction) place three motifs in such a way that in any row

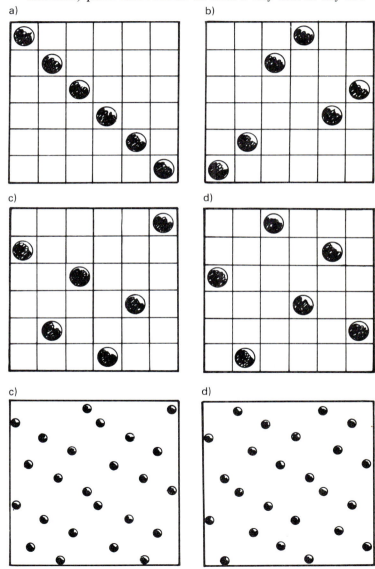

Fig. 3.25 The six-square unit showing various placements of the motif (a), (b), (c) and (d). Each will produce a different pattern in repeat. (c) and (d) are seen in repeat below

of squares in either direction, side to side, or top to bottom, only one square is occupied.

In the 4-square unit, four squares should be occupied in the same way, in the 5-square unit, five, and so on, bearing in mind that on any line in any direction, one square only should be occupied (see Fig. 3.24).

How these arrangements work in repeat can be seen by repeating the original subdivided unit (a photocopier can be useful here!) and removing the guidelines (see Fig. 3.25).

THEORY AND PRACTICE

Any textile design on paper is really just an exercise in textile theory, as the final design is always (hopefully) produced on cloth. In terms of fabric, and how it affects pattern, theory is no substitute for practice, and no amount of cutting or folding of paper will give a true impression of the design on cloth as it folds around the body, or hangs in drapes across a window. Even a panel print on a garment is not simply a picture. It becomes alive and moves with the form it encloses. Unlike screen-printed 'limited editions' on paper, with which it shares certain characteristics, the single panel print used on a garment is affected by many considerations that do not affect the picture that hangs flat against the wall.

As soon as (and before) textile designs are produced for a specific purpose, certain things must be taken into account.

Fig. 3.26   A directional design by Alison Hesketh

The final function of the fabric will determine the type of cloth used, the amount of colours to be printed, and the dimensions of the design. Certain types of design are difficult or expensive to produce commercially. Directional designs (ones in which all the dominant features face the same way up (Fig. 3.26) can prove costly to the garment manufacturer as they affect the lay of the dress pattern pieces when the garments are cut out *en masse*. A great deal of waste is created by the need for all the pattern pieces to face the same way – a flower that appears to grow up one sleeve cannot trail down the other! When a directional design is used for furnishing purposes it is slightly more practical as the fabric is often cut to hang one way, as curtains, or seat covers.

A deep repeat can also prove expensive to the customer. When lengths of cloth are cut into pieces as curtains a certain wastage occurs due to the fact that when joined side by side the lengths of fabric also have to be moved up or down each other to ensure that the repeat fits, and that large motifs occur in the right place. A deep repeat therefore creates more wastage than a shallow one.

A design which has a strong diagonal emphasis that might be successful in one situation could prove disastrous in another: it may give a flowing line when gathered on a garment, and yet lend a disconcerting slant to a wall on which it is hung as wallpaper. A colour that may be successful when applied to one situation may be totally unacceptable in another. Certain designs that involve the use of extremely expensive and sophisticated machinery may be totally wrong for the market which is served by this equipment. Some printing techniques may only be in common use in other countries. Some designs may involve the use of too many colours, or use so fine and tiny a repeat that they can only be produced by handscreen printing (very costly!). And then there are considerations of scale, cost, public or private taste, and fashion. The task (and pleasure) of the textile designer is to stretch all limitations of his field of design, and exploit the potential of pattern.

CHAPTER 4

Colour

The use of colour in textile design has its own magic and creates its own special problems and frustrations. It is influenced by many factors, some constant, and some that, at first, might seem arbitrary. Colour is the aspect of textile design that many students, when designing on paper, consider last, almost as an afterthought. Yet it is the single most powerful element at their disposal. Colour poses problems for the designer that are not shared by the 'fine' artist, and it is in the experience of colour that commercial textile design moves furthest away from painting. Colour is an emotive experience for the painter, in which objectivity and subjectivity both play their part. The painter is not influenced by production costs (except in so far as the cost of the production affects his own pocket), fashion, or the changing taste of the general public. He is free to do with colour what he will, and to exploit its effects unhampered by considerations which, to him, might appear irrelevant. It is these very factors which are of minimum interest to the painter, that are so vitally important to the commercial textile designer, who must constantly be aware of such factors as the psychological impact of colour, the importance of market research, and methods of trend forecasting, all of which can make or break a season's collection. A colour which is 'right' for the painter may incorporate a hundred variations upon that colour within one small area. He may employ the most delicate changes, or make the most subtle variations. He is the master of the colour he chooses.

The textile designer is not so fortunate. In the chain of people that links the designer to the public are many individuals who, in their different capacities, may find the opportunity to alter some aspect of a design as it passes through their hands – the buyer, the studio manager, the colourist, even the managing director's secretary – all may come into contact with the design once it leaves the designer's portfolio. The colour is the one aspect of a design that can be changed even at the last minute, and the effects of a colour combination that has taken months to refine can be destroyed in an instant by a well-intentioned colour mixer on the factory floor, to whom 'a red is just a red', and to whom extreme subtleties of colour do not exist.

The painter can utilise all the media available in search of the right colour – paints, pencils, inks, chalks, and even dyes. The textile designer may also make use of these media at the design stage, but must bear in mind how they most successfully imitate the effect of the printed cloth, and the similarity of their appearance to that of dyes and print pastes.

All the considerations that relate to the ultimate use of the cloth affect the choice and type of colour. They are of prime importance and should be considered at the earliest stages of production, when quite arbitrary motivations can cause the designer to pick up one colouring media or another. There are many influences that can affect the final appearance of the colour on the cloth, and not all of these relate to the colouring media used on paper. In a way, it is necessary to work (or at least think) backwards, as certain aspects of the final print may affect the media chosen to produce the original design. This can be important both to the commercial designer, who must have knowledge of the limitations that may be imposed upon him by industrial printing techniques, and to the designer-craftsman who may be required to produce a close facsimile of his own paper design on cloth. It is useful to know how certain dyes affect the fabric, how they may or may not be overprinted, how they may be reduced or thickened, and how these processes affect the final appearance of the colour and the feel of the cloth.

Some dyes are transparent like water-colour or ink, and can be thickened with gum without losing their luminosity. Others have an appearance like that of gouache; they sit on top of the cloth and bond to its surface. The designs on some fabrics are dyed, using highly sophisticated machinery, some are screen printed, some are roller printed, and some are transfer printed. Each method is suitable for a particular design or cloth.

A knowledge of various fabrics and how they function can be gained by experience, and is obviously of significance to the designer, as the surface of a cloth can influence the colour applied to it in different ways. Some fabrics can affect colour by absorption, some by reflection, and some by the interference of texture. Of the hundreds of fabrics available, there are those which are like velvet, deep and rich, with a pile that will absorb some dyes, and be, itself, absorbed or destroyed by other dyes. Some fabrics are paper-like – brittle silks or glazed cottons – other fabrics are rubbery and deceptive, their tooth cannot be felt on the surface, and yet it can be seen under a plastic coating. It can be covered and concealed by colour. Some fabrics are highly reflective, others suggest a moiré or watered effect, and yet others are as loosely woven as hessian or gauze. All these fabric surfaces influence the colour that is applied on to them, causing shadows and reflections which may enliven or deaden them. Certain fabrics may suggest certain types of colour to the designer, and experience shows that colours used on one surface that may look subtle and delicate, may appear drab or dull on another. So it is not surprising to learn that, primarily, it is the colour which sells a design. The use of colour can hasten the sale of a bad design and prevent the sale of a good one.

When buying, we all react instinctively to the colours we like or dislike, or those which, in our opinion (or the opinion of others) 'suit' us. Such reactions may be personal and individual, and grow from conditioning, or they may stem from the subconscious, where certain colours may be associated with past events, the significance of which is buried deep in the mind. Reactions to colour can also take the form of a collective preference for a certain type of colour, in that particular colours seem to be favoured by the population of particular countries. These national preferences are often conditioned by the climate and light, and it is not difficult to see how such preferences develop, associating, as we do, different colours with different seasons. The cool, natural, and clean colours of Scandinavian or Swedish textile design in the 1960s and 1970s suggested clearly the fresh, crisp, and airy climate of these countries. We only have to think of the Mediterranean climate to feel that sensation of saturated heat and light that produces such rich colours in the landscape and seascape. Only the earthy, misty, British weather could produce the subtle colours that are reflected in our fine British tweeds and Fair Isle knitwear. The strong colours produced with synthetic dyestuffs that are so popular with the African countries, and the powerful reds and oranges favoured by the Latins, can produce strong national antipathies in other, less fiery, temperaments.

The symbolism of colour is used world-wide to signify certain events or states of mind and spirit, and it must be recognised that the significance of a colour in one country may not be the same as the significance of the same colour in another country. A colour that may be used for a ceremony of life or rebirth in one culture may be seen as a symbol of death, and used during funerary occasions in another; in yet another, it may symbolise a season.

Colour also signifies political allegiances, national events, and religious and secular celebrations.

Conditioning has led us to respond to particular colours in a certain way. Often this reaction is spontaneous and immediate, and it is for this reason that some colours are used to give information, and more especially warnings, with more direct an impact than the written word. When driving, we stop at a red light, and advance at a green one. An amber light is less powerful than a red one, but in this situation it carries its own unspoken warning. We automatically associate a red road sign with a message to take notice, even before we read its actual wording.

In everyday language, colour terminology is used to describe mood, character, or circumstance. We speak of being 'in the pink' or 'having the blues'; being 'browned off', or green with envy.' We may speak of 'showing a red rag to a bull', or accuse someone of being 'yellow'. A person with a strong individual personality is often described as having a 'colourful character', or he may have a 'colourful past', about which he tells 'highly coloured' stories. In Britain, black is generally held to signify slightly sinister or mournful events; the black sheep, who is the outsider of the flock, or the black witch who deals in black magic, as opposed to the good 'white witch'. In the past, a rascally character was called a blackguard, and blackmail is held to be a particularly repugnant crime. One exception we may look forward to is when our bank account is in the black, and not in the red!

Colours can provoke a strong physical or psychological reaction. Certain colours may suggest weight or lightness; they may appear to advance and encroach, or to recede; and they can make us feel warm or cold, restful or agitated. The impressions of colour that we carry with us that register 'warm' or 'cold', and make us actually experience rises or drops in temperature due to the colour of our surroundings are a legacy that we have inherited from our forefathers who lived so close to the elements. We carry in our subconscious reactions to colour that are the result of centuries of mental imprints. Blue has come to symbolise the clear sky, sea, and summer. The coolness of blue makes it seem remote or detached. Red signifies danger, and green is associated with grass and the landscape and, as such, is found to induce feelings of peace and tranquillity.

Of all the considerations that affect colour in the area of textile design, fashion is the most intriguing. What is it that can make one colour that has been 'out' for many years, suddenly the height of fashion? Is it conscious planning by fashion designers? Is it the result of a natural cycle? Or is it simply chance? Fashions in colour come and go, and each cycle should be noted and understood by the designer. Fashions in furnishings may change more slowly than those in garments, but change they do, and it is important to keep abreast of developments in all the fields that may influence textile design. Painters, fashion designers, interior designers, illustrators, and sculptors, all have influenced textile design in the past and it is with the work of these artists that the textile designers should keep in contact. Sometimes these influences are only seen clearly in retrospect, but often a certain 'feeling' or style will recur throughout art and design that can point the way to the discerning designer. Often this takes the form of a trend towards the use of particular types of colour, and its origins sometimes lie with the 'fine' artists.

The textile artist/craftsman may feel himself to be outside the dictates of fashion, but is nevertheless influenced by it, albeit subconsciously. He is often commissioned by a private buyer who may be more fashion-conscious than he, or his work may be specifically bought to adorn a fashionable interior.

Just as a design may be placed chronologically, so will a colour conjure up a certain era, (see Fig. 4.1), and it may signify different things to different generations – the purple mourning taffetas and stiff dark silks of the Victorian age could not be further removed from the exotic dyed feather boas, purple miniskirts and 'granny' coats of Britain's 'Biba' era in the early 1970s. Yet the colours and the various types of fabric used during both periods were very similar in appearance.

The change in mood that can sweep a country, be it optimism, pessimism, conservatism, or patriotism can herald changes in fashion and colour trends. Royal occasions, new technological discoveries, world-wide events, and cinema and television – all have helped to promote and spread the acceptance of 'new' or unfamiliar colours, and have led to the redefinition of the position of 'old' or unfashionable ones. Cinema and television have shown us the life styles and homes of the famous and have helped to popularise colours and fashions. The arbiters of taste can quickly direct the public to a re-evaluation of hitherto unacceptable or unfashionable colours and styles, and each generation and group looks to its own idols for guidance. A colour that once may have seemed dull or oppressive in the eyes of 'the public' may be seen, in the home of a movie star, to be rich and opulent (complemented, as it is, by the trappings of success). Conversely, an interior that once would have seemed cold and clinical is suddenly found to be 'pristine' or 'minimal' when seen afresh through the eyes of television and media hype, and

Fig. 4.1 Style and colour make it easy for us to place a design chronologically.
(a) 'Wandle', by William Morris, 1884

suddenly a new style is born – 'High-tech'.*

Technology has given us new cloths, new dyes, and novel textures. We have used synthetic dyestuffs to create garish and luminous colours and to imitate natural earth colours. In our own time fashion has placed these colours where they seem to belong: luminous colours in the disco, and 'natural' colours in

*'High-tech' was a distinctive style of furnishing and interior design fashionable from 1980, in which industrial and commercial fittings were utilised and adapted for use in the domestic interior.

(b) 'Calyx', by Lucienne Day,
1951

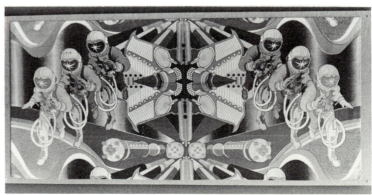

(c) 'Spacewalk', by Sue Palmer,
1969. Warner and Sons Ltd.
Copyright © 1983

the homes of the conservation conscious, where the colours and textures of earth and wood seem to symbolise a return to pollution-free living. Passing trends have seen the 'jazz' colours of the 1950s; the psychedelic colour combinations of the drug-induced trip in the 1960s, and all the maroons, mustards, khakis, and baby-doll pinks that we would not dream of putting next to our skin were they not in fashion. Yet it seems that each time a colour comes back into vogue it looks new. Different accessories, the distribution of colour and its proximity to other colours, and many other factors, can make a colour appear to us in a way in which we feel we have not seen it before. Each generation that grows up with an interest in fashion has its own allegiances to colour. Old prejudices may fade, but others surely take their place. We may not believe today that 'Blue and green should never be seen without another colour in between', but nevertheless the place of this myth has been taken by other preconceptions that give a hint as to the continuing conformity of our customers. Even though, today, 'anything goes', the 'anything' the 'goes' is, in fact, just a tiny part of all the options that are open to the designer, and, speaking of colour, it is not surprising to learn of the very few colours that are usable in the fashion market at any particular time. The mass market can be very unpredictable, as many a manufacturer knows to his cost.

However, there may be constants – some colours may recur, in one form or another each year, or may be conspicuous by their continued absence. Certain types of colour may occur seasonally because of their practicality in certain weather. Others may be perennially popular with a certain age-group, due to preconceptions of 'smartness'.

Colour predictions are issued regularly, and it will be seen that some colours rarely appear within any grouping. It may be that they have been found, from past experience, to be unpopular to such a degree that it has been thought expedient to use them only in a way in which their sale is assured, or to introduce them slowly in a subtle or muted form, to be strengthened as they become more familiar, and thus more acceptable.

It is unusual for pastel shades to form the basis of a winter fashion collection – it would simply not be practical. However, pastel shades can be used as accessory colours with the intention of adding a touch of sparkle or lightness to a dark or sombre collection. Conversely, dark colours are rarely used as the basis of a summer collection. Light colours are more comfortable in the heat as they reflect more light, and they produce a feeling of airiness and weightlessness that we feel we need in bright strong sunlight. There are (we hope!)

no rain or mud splashes to spoil them, so light bright colours are the obvious summer choice. Just as light colours seem to weigh less, so darker colours give us the reassurance of warmth and depth that we need in winter. A particular pale blue may be tinted with black to grey it and make it seem more wintry; with red or orange, to warm it and give it a hint of autumn; or with white, to cool it. Mix it with proportions of, or place it next to, other colours, and it changes again, and changes them in turn. Minor modifications in the proportion of constituent colours can produce a myriad of tones, shades, tints, hues, one or more of which may be suitable for one season or another.

'Colour theory' is often taught as a separate subject in art schools, and there are many excellent books which deal explicitly with the theory of colour. Once the basic knowledge has been acquired the individual can exploit colour towards his or her own ends.

You will find that there are only three pure colours – red, yellow and blue – that cannot be made from other colours. These are termed the primaries. From these, are made the secondary colours: orange, green, and violet. Mixing these together in different proportions, plus black, white, or grey produces a range of colours and tones that is infinite.

The terminology of colour theory can confuse as well as aid – even more so when the terms used in colour theory are applied to textile design, which uses its own terminology for colouring processes. However, as most textile designs are sold in the form of a design painted on paper, the designer must work in one medium with ultimate reference to another, and to understand that the design on paper is an interpretation, in advance, of the final product.

Whether in dyes or paints, the most intense colours are the primaries. Each of these may be combined with both the others, to produce a 'non-colour' a kind of brown/black. Dual combinations of secondary colours will produce tertiaries: orange and violet will yield a soft red; green and violet a soft blue; and orange and green a soft tan. The exact hue will depend upon the proportions of the colours that have been mixed together. Mixtures of golden yellow and vermilion in varying proportions will create a range of strong oranges. Turquoise blue and lemon yellow will combine to produce a range of yellow greens, and crimson will result in a range of purples when mixed with ultramarine. Tints result when white is mixed with a colour; shades, when black is mixed with it; and tones when grey is mixed with it. Good-quality artists' gouache should be used when mixing precise colours so that standard results are obtained.

Yet while the standards of colour theory remain constant, the names that we give to fashionable colours come and go. Although it is possible to guarantee an exact colour mix by referring to numbered colour charts, we still react with enthusiasm to the associations conjured up by such names as old gold, emerald green, shocking pink, battleship grey, grape, wine, air force blue, marigold, and sand.

A colour is rarely seen in isolation against a white ground. It reacts differently, depending on surrounding colours. It may appear to flicker, to distort the shape which contains it, or it may lose or gain in intensity, so strongly is it influenced by the colours that surround it. A light colour appears more important against a dark ground, and more insignificant against a pale one. A small area of one colour in the right relationship to another can make as much impact as a large area of the same colour seen in isolation. Certain combinations of colour can make the eye and the brain work overtime, creating optical illusions and after-images. Different tones can be used to create effects such as geometric shapes and tile patterns that can seem three-dimensional, and that play disconcerting tricks when seen on a horizontal surface (see Fig. 4.2).

We have learned from the natural world to use colour as camouflage. The patterned, flecked, or dappled coats or bodies of animals and birds blend perfectly with their habitat, sometimes changing as their surroundings change. Although the flecked carpets that we use to defy the effects of wear and tear do not actually change in the way a chameleon does, nevertheless they do camouflage dust and grit, and are often

Fig. 4.2 (a) 'Three-dimensional' pattern can play disconcerting tricks on the eye when seen on a flat surface

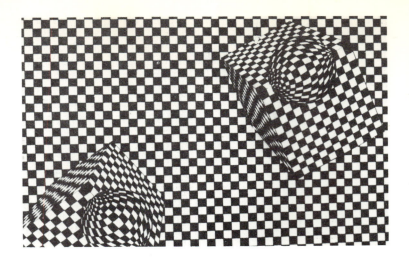

Fig. 4.2 (b) 'Three-dimensional' pattern can play disconcerting tricks on the eye when seen on a flat surface

designed for this purpose. Textured or randomly patterned and coloured wall coverings can camouflage an uneven wall surface. Certain colours can 'camouflage' or apparently alter the shape of the human figure, hence the fact that fashion writers have advised plump people not to wear loud colours. The term 'camouflage' describes the type of pattern and colour that renders the wearer indistinguishable from his or her surroundings. The camouflage clothing that was designed for jungle warfare, surfaces now and again as street fashion, where it becomes simply another surface pattern when removed from its special environment. Camouflage only exists as part of its habitat – the butterfly, which is part of a highly coloured pattern among the flowers, becomes a bright jewel as it flies away (Fig. 4.3).

Camouflage can be used in many different ways in textile design. It is possible to change the texture of the cloth, or parts of it, by covering it with a dense pigment print-paste. A design can be camouflaged by the use of colour – very closely related tones or shades can so disguise the edges of pattern that, at a distance, the pattern appears not to exist, and the all-over effect is one of a plain, but subtly changing surface. This effect is sometimes used on wallpapers or furnishings that are intended to be used in small rooms or narrow areas. The pattern is 'felt' without encroaching or intruding into its surroundings (see Fig. 4.4a).

Often a design will be produced that has two distinct aspects, such as a geometric design that appears to exist on two separate levels, one beneath the other, neither of which have a link with the other that brings them on to the same

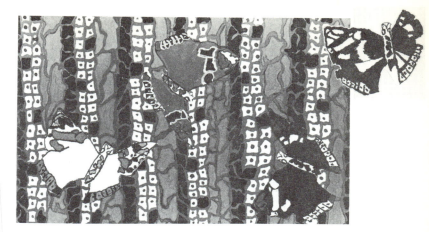

Fig. 4.3 'Natural camouflage.'
Design by Gillian Coates

Fig. 4.4 Tone can be used to
play up, or play down the impact
of a design. Design by Selena
Forrest

level. A floral design may sometimes 'sit' on top of a sub-pattern which is used as a kind of subtle background texture. In these types of design colour can be used to emphasise one level, and camouflage another, with the result that the two patterns do not vie for equal attention. On the other hand, colour can also be used to emphasise the subtle layering of similar shapes that forms a design that only just appears to exist on two levels. (see Fig. 4.5).

In the design of textiles camouflage is always used in this way, to different degrees. One part of a design is often 'camouflaged' or played down to the advantage of another, to avoid the lack of emphasis that would result were all elements afforded the same value.

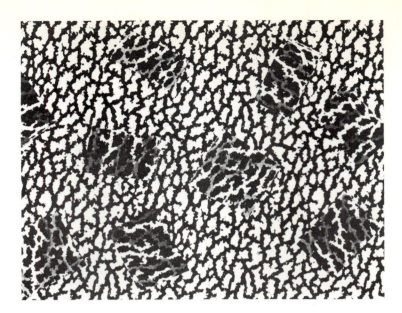

Fig. 4.5 Colour can be used to emphasise shapes in a design that only just appears to be on two levels. Design by Belinda Blackwell

The question of colour and emphasis is one that is of prime importance when producing colourways. A colourway is a small part of the design produced in a set of colours that are different from the original, but retain the original emphasis. A commercially printed fabric is usually produced in at least four colourways, and it is sometimes the responsibility of the designer to present the colourways as well as the design. Many companies who have their own studios employ colourists to work specifically in this area. The colourist works from the original design, balancing colour for colour, and shade for shade, ensuring that the rhythms of the original design are repeated in the colourways. It is important that the original appeal of the design is retained throughout the colourways. Take, for example, a design of bright green leaves growing up a pale pink trellis, set against a deep navy blue background. Both the leaves and the trellis advance from the background – the trellis because it is pale against a dark ground, the leaves because they are bright against a dark ground. If in one colourway the ground was pale, the overall effect of the design would be radically different. The trellis would fade into the background, and some of the luminous effect of the leaves would be lost. In this instance, therefore, a dark background should be retained throughout all the colourways, and all the tonal values should also be the same in each colourway.

Students often disregard the importance of the background of a design, feeling that it can be changed at any point during production – dark substituted for light, light for dark, coloured for uncoloured. In fact the reverse is actually the case, and it must be remembered that the background is an intrinsic part of the design, and that to change it from white to a colour not only alters the design but involves an extra printing process, and therefore entails a greater cost.

The rhythms and focal points of a design must be carefully planned during the early stages, using groups of colours distributed in different ways to suggest the dominant features. The actual number of elements in any design determine the possible emphases. Emphasis by definition suggests the 'playing up' of one (or a small number) of elements, the importance of which is stressed by its relationship to the others. If all the elements within a design are afforded the same value in colour, i.e. if the colours used are of the same strength or tone, and arranged across the design equally in proportionate amounts, no one element will appear more important than another, no rhythms will be reinforced, and the limited effect of such a colour scheme will be equally evident in further colourways.

Distribution and proportion of colour are of vital importance when applied to commercial textile design. Because furnishing fabric is often hung in large expanses, or used to cover three-dimensional objects, the cumulative effect of a bright or luminous colour can be compounded to such a degree that the fabric becomes unbearable to live with. That little spot of acid green pigment flickering in the centre of a scarlet painting can take on oppressive new life when multiplied to form a pattern distributed evenly over a large red area, or when spread as a solid colour over an expanse of curtaining or wallpaper.

Thus it follows that because the power of colour depends, to a degree, on its surroundings, small amounts of colour can be as efficiently used as large amounts. Impact does not necessarily depend upon quantity. Small spots of colour twinkle against a dark ground; a pale shape against a pale ground is 'lifted' or emphasised by a dark or powerful colour used around it as an outline. Similarly, a light outline can separate a dark shape from its dark ground, and small areas of white can give life or sparkle to a matt cloth that is covered in printed pattern.

Secondary or tertiary colours can be radically changed by minor modifications made to their component colours. The effect of complementary colours which, when used together, may appear too violent, can be made more restful by adding proportions of grey or white to one or both of them. A small proportion of green added to a strong vermilion will create a deep, rich tan, and a bitter acid yellow will move towards a subtle olive green if black is added to it. The impact of a colour can also be altered by the construction of the cloth, and its weight and texture. A finely woven gauze or organdie may be dyed the same colour as a densely woven cotton sateen, but the effects of light and shade, weight, transparency, and reflectiveness each give the colour a different appearance. The same colour can appear soft, hard, brash, misty, reflective, practical, or fun, depending upon the cloth it covers, and the associations that we make with various fabrics. In textile design, proportion is a delicate balance between cloth construction, surface, scale, and distribution of pattern and colour.

You, as textile designer or craftsman, may produce items that exist in their own right as works of art, and are intended to be hung on the pristine white walls of an art gallery. Conversely, you may produce work that is specifically designed to be displayed or used in a domestic or municipal setting. A piece may be part of a planned colour scheme, or its focal point. You will use colour with different intentions at different times to suit a brief that you may have set yourself, or that may have been set for you. You may use it to exploit an idea or a technique, to set a mood, to express an emotion, to illustrate a theory, to suggest form or light, or simply for the joy of it. In whichever direction that your work takes you, you will, at all stages, encounter the intriguing problems posed by colour. Colour can be the most fascinating aspect of textile design. It can destroy a good design, and resurrect a bad one. It can create illusions, and it can set moods, and influence moods. The use of colour will make many demands upon you, and reveal many delightful surprises.

CHAPTER 5

Screen printing

You, as a student, are in the enviable position of being able to produce work totally for own satisfaction. This happy situation will eventually come to an end, but for the time being you are free to follow your own lines of investigation, unhampered by any considerations other than those of personal choice.

This very freedom and opportunity to develop personal ideas can sometimes leave you feeling frustrated, owing to the fact that you feel you have produced designs that are in advance of the equipment you are using. Conversely, if you have sophisticated equipment at your disposal, you may feel obliged to design to make use of it, believing if you produce simple designs, and use the most basic equipment, that your designs somehow are not 'good' enough. Nevertheless, the most simple ideas are often the most successful, especially on fabric, and the most basic equipment need not necessarily produce the most uninteresting results. You only have to look at traditional batiks to realise the results that can be produced with the basic tools (see Fig. 7.1).

Even with the simplest equipment at your disposal you have access to a wide variety of techniques; and yet even then, it is craftsmanship and a good design sense that will produce the best results. The beauty of designer-made craft textiles is that they cannot be produced by machine; use machinery and equipment to your own ends, but remember, it is your own talent that counts. In any case, textile media are extremely versatile, and it is possible to create many different effects with the most simple tools. It is the ideas that are important after all, and things can be as simple or as complicated as you want them to be.

You can adapt your designs to suit the process you are using, or, to some degree, choose the process that suits your designs. Should you need such equipment as light boxes, steamers, screens, and screen exposure units, these can all be made on a reduced scale for use in the small workshop. Many of the materials recommended can also be bought in small quantities.

Fig. 5.1 Japanese stencils: the print-paste is pushed through the open (white) areas with a soft brush

You personally may have the most limited or the most varied facilities available. You may have the use of high-pressure steamers, bakers, mechanised dye vats, and photographic and reproductive equipment. Your college may even employ technicians who will print entire lengths of fabric for you, so that you do not see your design again until it is complete on cloth. On the other hand, you may be forced to work with the most basic equipment, and even that important commodity, time, may be is short supply.

Fortunately, not all print processes are time-consuming. Many can be broken down into definite stages, and it is this feature that makes them so easy to understand.

You need not be daunted either by dye recipes or fixing methods, complicated measurements, or lengthy preparation. Not all dyes are difficult to use – some are easily mixed, and equally easy to fix. There are dyes to suit every situation and fabric.

Most common processes can be adapted to suit individual requirements. You can work in a 'domestic' setting, using basic equipment to simulate industrial methods if you wish. You can keep in touch with actual developments in the textile industry by visiting printworks, arranging work experience with studios where possible, and constantly carrying out your own 'market research'. You can draw the line between craft and commerce wherever you please, taking from each world what you need, and giving to each what you feel you have to offer.

For textile students, the pleasure actually comes from designing *and* printing the fabric, and this affords the ideal opportunity to use a variety of media and techniques.

Each technique used in the decoration of textiles has its own characteristics. However, one aspect that most of them have in common is that they are basically forms of resist, in that only parts of the cloth are printed. Other parts of the cloth are either treated to resist the dye, or else the dye is prevented from touching them by some other means. In batik, wax or starch is applied to parts of the fabric, in bandhana (tie-dye), parts of the cloth are bound tightly to resist the dye, and in screen printing, parts of the screen mesh are covered or blocked to prevent the print-paste passing through. The beauty of tie-dye, batik, and hand painting, is that the results are not exactly repeatable. The beauty of screen printing is that they are. Once the preliminary processes are complete, the design can be reproduced *ad infinitum*. Although cylindrical screens are often used in the textile industry today, the closest parallel that the student has to industrial methods is the flat screen. Using this, coupled with a basic range of dyes, fabrics, and facilities, prints can be produced that are professional-looking, and of a high quality.

FROM STENCIL TO SCREEN

As children, most of us have used stencils, repeating shapes by pushing colour through holes cut in pieces of card. Some stencils were more complicated than others, comprised of shapes that were held inside the open areas by thin 'bars' of the card. The bars of card were often incorporated into the design and in any event could not be removed, as they prevented the stencil falling apart. The need for such ties meant that free, unattached shapes were not possible.

However, stencils need not be so basic: the extremely complex and sophisticated results that are possible using stencils can be seen in the work produced by the Japanese, who developed the art of stencilling to a peak of excellence, and who still use stencils today. The Japanese artists refined the interconnecting stencil bars more and more until ties of human hair or silk were used. Such ties were so fine as to be almost invisible, yet strong enough to hold free, or floating shapes in position (see Fig. 5.2).

Stencils are used to produce a positive, or a negative image – positive when dye paste is pushed through, and a negative when a resist paste is used. In the latter case, the fabric is later dyed, and the resist paste removed, leaving the pattern clear (see Fig. 8.15). Designs of more than one colour can also be produced. Each colour is cut out of its own stencil, and the stencils are then placed on the cloth one by one in register, leaving a complete design when the final colour has been applied.

Today we use screens, which are a direct development of the stencil. The place of the silk ties has been taken by the screen mesh, on to which the stencil is fixed or transferred. The design is colour-separated in basically the same way, each colour having its own stencil and screen.

It is surprising to realise that stencilling has been carried out in Japan from the eighth century, and yet screen printing was not developed as an industry in Europe until the 1920s!

Screen printing on fabric became popular for many reasons. It was quicker than block and roller printing, (which were the methods of fabric printing in common use at the time) and the cost of setting up a design was not so great. Freer and more spontaneous designs were possible using screens, and this aspect of screen printing appealed to the

Fig. 5.2 An enlarged Japanese stencil shows clearly the fine threads that are used to hold delicate parts of the stencil together

artists of the day, who were quick to dabble in it. The freedom of screen printing ideally suited the designs and dyes being produced at this time for the new synthetic fabrics, and in this situation, in countries that were ripe for change, screen printing was eminently suitable.

It is for many of these reasons that screen-printing processes are used so much in schools and colleges today. Multicoloured repeating designs can be produced on fabric relatively quickly, using screens and stencils of various types, many of which have changed little over the years. Although methods of screen printing in the textile *industry* have changed, professional-looking fabrics can still be produced in the college or home environment using surprisingly unsophisticated equipment.

EQUIPMENT

If necessary, the basic equipment for screen printing can be very basic indeed. It is possible to print on a kitchen table, using paper stencils and home-made screens and squeegees.

Although the student usually has more resources available, it may nevertheless be necessary for him to gather his own equipment together in the future. In some cases this may mean actually constructing it. Fortunately, a middle course can be steered, with the readily available or cheaper pieces of equipment being bought, and the more expensive pieces being made or adapted. Directions follow for the construction or the composition of such things as print tables and light boxes. Smaller items such as squeegees are relatively cheap to buy. Alternatives to expensive materials are given where possible, as specialist surfaces such as those used on commercial print tables are very expensive.

Print tables

Commercial print tables vary in length from 3 m sample tables, upwards. (In some industrial methods a table is not used at all, the rotary screens being placed one above the other, or one beside the other, while the fabric moves against them.)

For 'domestic' purposes, the size of the print table depends upon the space that is available. In theory (and often in practice!) any flat table can be used for printing. A printing surface can be made easily, and a complete table can be built if a permanent site is available. For well-fitting repeats and good colour registration, however, a purpose-built print table is really needed.

A commercial print table has a durable rubber surface on to which the fabric can be glued to hold it flat during printing. It also has a registration rail which is made of steel, and precision set in alignment with the table. Good registration is ensured by a series of movable metal stops that can be locked in position on the rail. A bracket, fixed to each screen, rests against a stop at every repeat (see Fig. 5.30).

Although the main problem with a home-made print table is one of registration, it is possible to register screens on such a table if care is taken to position the screens accurately.

Bearing in mind that the craftsman may simply want the best printing surface, and may not necessarily be concerned with repeat, a perfectly adequate table can be easily made:

Cloth-covered table-top
1. Obtain a sheet of blockboard approximately 2 cm thick (the thicker the better) and cut to the size you require. (If you plan to print lengths of fabric, this will be approximately 3 m long.) If possible, permanent legs should be attached, and the table should be firm and resilient.

2. Lay a layer of dense sponge or foam rubber (e.g. carpet underlay) on to the blockboard, pull it flat, and attach it firmly with drawing-pins or staples.
3. Stretch one or two blankets over the sponge, and fix them in the same way.
4. Stretch at least three layers of calico over the blankets, fixing each individually, and avoiding wrinkles. The final surface should be soft but firm.

A special rubber print-table top can be purchased. While it is expensive it can be a time-saving investment, as well as helping to produce better prints.

Pinning and gumming

There are several different ways in which the fabric can be fixed to the table for printing. Whenever possible, gumming is to be preferred. It is more efficient and holds the cloth tighter, preventing it swelling and contracting so much during printing. Gum is available which is suitable for sticking fabric to a rubber surface (see UK suppliers, p. 241). It is possible to fix most fabrics to the table in this way, but in practice it is sometimes found that a fabric is more suitable for pinning than gumming. Some synthetics are difficult to stick down, and various other fabrics which are very fine must be pinned to a back-cloth. This absorbs excess print-paste that would otherwise bleed back into the fabric from the non-absorbent rubber. A back-cloth should consist of a substantial calico, or a pure, heavy cotton. The back-cloth is ironed to the print table, and can be left in position throughout many prints. It should be ironed with a hot iron after each completed print to fix any colour that has come through from the printed fabric.

When using a home-made print table, pinning is the only choice, as fabric cannot be glued to the calico surface. (If a rubber surface has been fixed to the table, obviously the fabric *can* be gummed.)

The procedure for pinning is similar, whether pinning into a back-cloth, or into a cloth-covered home-made table. The main difference lies in the angle at which the pins are inserted. When using a cloth-covered table, the pins must be pushed in at a 45° angle. When pinning into a back-cloth, they must be pushed in horizontally to lie between the back-cloth and the rubber table-top. On no account must they be allowed to pierce the rubber.

Pinning procedure

1. Lay the fabric on the table in the correct position for printing. (If a registration bar is being used for purposes of

Fig. 5.3 Pinning

repeat, this measurement will have previously been written on the screen (p. 113).

2. Measure the distance from the registration bar to the edge of the fabric, or the edge of the table to the edge of the fabric, as the case may be. Checking the measurement as you go, and pulling the fabric taut, pin it down along the selvage at about 3 cm intervals.

3. Now smooth the fabric flat, so that the crossgrain of the cloth is square with the selvage. Stand at the middle of the opposite selvage, pull the fabric taut, and insert one or two pins to hold it (see Fig. 5.3).

4. Working out from the centre to one side, pin the selvage, pulling the fabric towards you, and pulling it taut along the table at the same time. Make sure that the edge of the fabric is not pulled so tight that it forms a scalloped edge. The finished corner should be in line with the opposite corner, ensuring that the grain of the fabric is straight.

5. Work outwards from the centre to the other corner.

6. Pin the two ends of the cloth, pulling just tight enough to hold them straight.

7. Cover the pins with a line of tape, to prevent them piercing the screen during printing.

Gumming procedure (rubber-covered tables only)

1. Using a squeegee, spread the gum over the table to form a fine film. Do not leave excess blobs or ridges of gum on the table. The gum can be dried with a fan set to 'cool', but heat should not be applied at this stage.

2. The fabric is ironed down with an iron set to 'cotton heat' for thick fabrics and 'wool heat' for thin fabrics. Lay the fabric on the table at the relevant distance from the bar or table edge, and iron carefully along the nearest selvage.

3. Return to the centre of the table, and place the iron in the middle of the selvage. Making a fan-shaped movement, iron a line of cloth above the first line of ironing, working first out to one corner, then out from the centre to the other.

4. Continue ironing in this way, always starting from the centre, and smoothing the fabric away from you and along as you iron. Minor creases can be gently lifted, and reironed.

Screens

For college or domestic purposes, screens can be made, or can be bought from suppliers. Metal or wooden screens can be used. Both types of screen are adequate, provided that they are stretched tightly enough. Wooden screens can be stretched by

Fig. 5.4 A dress screen with the above *inside* measurements allows space at top and bottom for a dye-well, and at either side of a 61 cm deep design

hand; metal screens must be stretched mechanically.

The dimensions of screens vary, ranging from small ones that hold just one motif, to large furnishing-width screens. The size of the screen is very important when deciding upon the repeat depth, and width of the design. As a guide, Fig. 5.4 shows the *inside* measurement of a screen to be used for printing dress fabrics (which are generally 90 cm wide). The frame should be made from lengths of approximately 5 × 4 cm wood, larger screens being made of slightly thicker wood. The screens should be well jointed at the corners, and perfectly flat. Screens that are poorly made or too thin will pull out of shape when the mesh is fixed to them, or will buckle and warp when wet.

Screen mesh

Originally, fine silk was used as screen mesh. Organdie was also found to be practical, although it has now been replaced by Terylene meshes which are more hard-wearing, and less fragile.

For experimental purposes, trials can be made with various types of Terylene voile. Terylene voile is tough and long lasting; however, if hand stretched, it does have a tendency to sag when wet, and although it dries taut, this feature obviously makes it an unsuitable base for permanent stencils.

Screen-process suppliers market special Terylene screen meshes which are stable, durable, and available in different grades, denoting density of weave. Each supplier uses his own system of classification. One system used is 'TT' – the higher the number, the finer the mesh, 8TT being a wide mesh. A medium mesh is suitable for most types of work. Designs that incorporate fine lines, fine dots, or a photographic half-tone, require a fine mesh. A fine mesh is also most suitable for diagonal lines that are to be exposed on to a screen photographically. Such lines often develop a 'saw' edge where they cross the weave of the mesh diagonally, and a fine mesh helps minimise this effect. Although Terylene mesh is expensive, it is very practical, as it can be cleared many times and reused. Also, large screens that are badly blocked or damaged can be stripped of mesh, which can then be cut down, and the clean areas used to cover smaller screens.

Stretching screens by hand

The screen, whether stretched by machine or by hand, should be as tight as a drum. The grain of the mesh must be straight, and parallel with the edge of the frame. The stretching procedure is as follows.

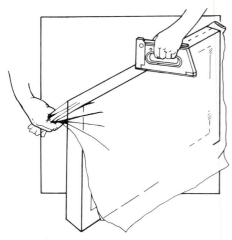

Fig. 5.5 Stretching a screen by hand: keep the staples parallel to the frame edge, and keep the grain of the mesh 'square' to the frame.

1. Cut the mesh a good 7 cms larger than the frame.
2. Fold the selvage under for added strength and, holding the frame upright, place the mesh on the frame in the position shown in Fig. 5.5.
3. Place the first staple in one corner so that the staple lies parallel to the frame.
4. Staple the mesh along the frame to the other corner, pulling it taut as you go, and keeping the folded edge of the mesh parallel to the edge of the frame.
5. Turn the screen upside-down, and checking that the grain of the mesh is straight, pull the mesh tight, and staple the corner as before.
6. Pulling the mesh along and across the frame, place a second staple about 3 cm away from the first, and continue tensioning and stapling to the other corner.
7. Turn the screen again, and staple the third edge, this time only pulling the mesh moderately tight.
8. The fourth edge must be pulled as tight as possible while being stapled in the usual way. The grain of the mesh must be kept 'square' to the frame.

Excess mesh must be folded under and stapled to the frame, to avoid ends unravelling that might later trail in the print-paste during printing.

A second row of staples can be added all round for extra strength if required, and a thin coating of spirit-based glue should be added to the face of the frame. (The 'face' is the edge that comes into contact with the table.)

If the screen is to be used for printing without a permanent stencil attached, it should be degreased by washing with a liquid detergent, washing-up liquid, or a degreasing agent. It should then be edged with brown-paper tape (Gumstrip).

Gumstripping

A gummed brown-paper tape, approximately 5 cm wide is used to seal the edges of the screen. Lengths of gumstrip, cut to the size of the frame, are dampened with a sponge, and stuck on to the face side of the frame, covering the join between frame and mesh (see Fig. 5.6). This prevents seepage of print-paste during printing. (*Note*: If a photographic stencil or a cut stencil is being used, the gumstrip should be applied *after* the stencil is put on the screen.)

A lining of tape can be stuck to the inside of the frame if required, although this is not strictly necessary. However, should an inside layer of tape be used, it should be creased along the middle, and pushed well down into the join between

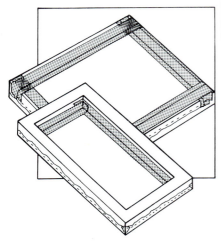

Fig. 5.6 Gumstrip is used to seal the join between the edge of the frame and the screen mesh

the frame and the mesh, and into the corners. Any pieces of tape left sticking out, or any parts not stuck down properly, are likely to be pulled off accidentally during printing.

The tape can be varnished to make it waterproof, the varnish being taken slightly over the edge of the tape on to the screen mesh.

Squeegees

The squeegee is the implement used to force the print-paste through the screen mesh. It is basically a flat piece of wood into which a rubber blade has been inserted. A squeegee can be made by buying a rubber blade and trapping it between two bars of wood. The wooden part must be varnished to make it waterproof, and long nails or handles should be fixed to either end of it, to prevent the squeegee slipping back into the print-paste during printing (see Fig. 5.7). The squeegee should be long enough to cover the depth of the design, but short enough to move freely across the screen without touching the edges of the frame.

When buying a squeegee it is important to buy one that is specifically intended for use on fabric, as squeegees have different blades for different purposes. The squeegee blade should always be kept free from particles of dried print-paste. It should be treated with respect and not allowed to become warped or dented, as this will result in uneven printing. When necessary, the blade can be resharpened (or smoothed) with fine glasspaper or sandpaper. The sandpaper should not be rubbed against the blade, but fixed to a flat surface, and the squeegee blade moved against it. This will ensure an even angle on the blade.

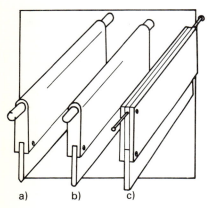

a)   b)   c)

Fig. 5.7   Squeegees:
(a) A pointed blade for fine lines
(b) A rounded blade for printing large open areas
(c) A flat blade for printing paper

Light boxes

A light box is very useful to the textile designer. It is used for preparing and retouching photographic stencils, and is invaluable when putting designs into repeat. For the purpose of checking repeats the light box must be considerably larger than the design, although a smaller light box can be used for touching up photographic stencils, as they can be moved around freely, and small areas checked one at a time. Photographic stencils can be checked against *any* light source – for example, against a window.

A permanent light box can be made by fixing a sheet of heavy frosted plate glass over a set of lights, or a temporary one can be made by simply resting a sheet of thick Perspex on sturdy supports over a light source.

Photographic exposure units

A photographic exposure unit is the means by which a design is exposed on to a screen that has previously been coated with light-sensitive liquid. A certain type of ultraviolet light is used for screen exposure (sunlight even can be used). The length of exposure depends upon the type and power of the lighting. One type of commercial exposure unit consists of an ultraviolet light box that incorporates a vacuum. The vacuum holds the photo stencil in contact with the screen against the light source, while also protecting the eyes against the harmful ultraviolet rays. Exposure times are supplied with such units.

Home-made exposure units can be successful, but *should be handled with extreme care. Ultraviolet light from an artificial light source should not be allowed to come into contact with either skin or eyes.* Lamps that project ultraviolet light on the right wavelength are available from screen-process suppliers, and care should be taken to fit them in accordance with the supplier's directions. The number of lights used, and exposure times, can be discovered by experience only, but as a guide, four 125 W 'mercury vapour' lamps could be used to project the minimum amount of light sufficient to expose a dress screen. One screen can be used to check exposure times, by giving parts of it increased lengths of time under the lights. The correct timing will be discovered when the screen is washed out. (The coating should be strong and solid after washing, and the open areas of mesh clear and unblocked.)

To avoid eye contact with the lights, they should be built into a complete unit with vertical sides that are deeper than the lights. This unit is suspended above the screen at the appropriate height. The screen rests under the unit on a flat surface. To take the place of a vacuum, good contact is maintained between the stencil material (usually Kodatrace; see 'Stencils,' below) and the screen mesh by means of the following: a piece of foam rubber cut to the inside measurement of, and deeper than, the frame, is painted black. The screen is placed over this, which raises it slightly from the table. The Kodatrace is taped to the screen, and a sheet of heavy plate glass rests on top (see Fig. 5.8). Needless to say, exposure units should be kept in a darkened room.

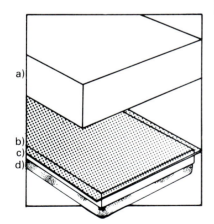

Fig. 5.8 A home-made exposure unit.
(a) A deep-sided construction containing ultraviolet lights
(b) A sheet of heavy plate glass
(c) The screen
(d) A piece of dense sponge (painted black on one side)

Washing troughs and bleach baths

An area should be set aside to serve as a wash-off. If emulsion-coated screens have been used for photographic exposure, a bleach bath will also be needed.

Screens must be washed off after printing in an area which allows enough space for them to be freely hosed. For small screens, a large sink or bath may be used; for larger screens, a special trough in which the screen can stand upright can be purpose built. Alternatively, a shower unit can be used. In fact, any construction is suitable that allows water to be hosed on to the screen, and to drain away freely. The wash-off should have sides which are deep enough to prevent spillage of water.

Bleach is used to remove certain screen coatings. A bleach bath is simply a container in which screens are left to soak in bleach and water. It can be constructed from an old screen frame and a sheet of heavy-duty polythene, or it can be purpose built in plastic, or brick and tile. (Running water is obviously an advantage, but home-made bleach baths do not necessarily need to be sited near a water supply.) As a quantity of bleach is used, it is recommended that several screens be bleached at once and, if possible, a permanent site be found for the bleach bath, to avoid the necessity of frequent emptying and refilling, and to save unneccesary expense.

STENCILS

There are several different types of stencil used in fabric printing, all of which, as stencils, incorporate the use of solid areas which block the mesh, and open areas which allow print-paste through.

The choice of stencil is determined by several different factors, as each has its own characteristics that make it suitable for some designs and not for others.

Some stencils are formed by painting a liquid block-out directly on to parts of the screen, some by the use of a 'photographic' screen coating, and some are actually cut by hand out of a stencil material, which is then fixed to the screen mesh by ironing.

As the print-paste used in fabric printing is water based, the substance that forms the screen stencil must be resistant to water. Anything that will resist water for a time can be used as a 'stencil', either to print through, or to print around (as in the case of actual objects placed under the screen, see Fig. 5.40).

The two stencils most commonly used in schools today for repeating designs are the knife-cut type (trade name: 'Profilm' or 'Stenplex Amber') and the photographic type: trade name 'Kodatrace' or 'Permatrace'.

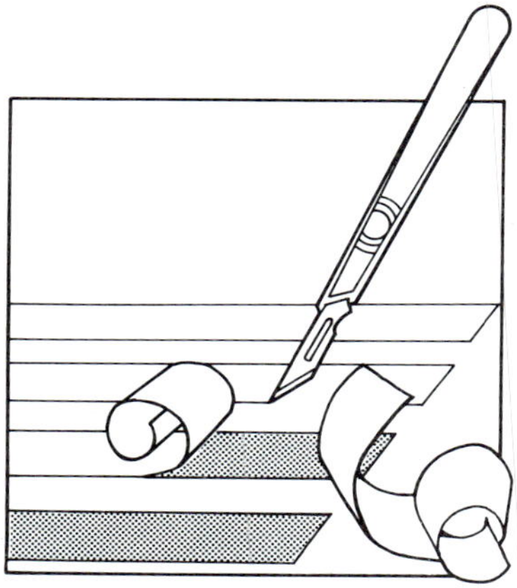

Knife-cut stencils

The knife-cut stencil is the form which is closest to the original type of stencil developed by the Japanese, the delicate threads that supported the design having evolved into a mesh on to which the stencil is eventually fixed.

In this case the stencil material takes the form of greaseproof paper with a brittle shellac coating. The image that is to be printed is cut into the coating and the shape peeled away from its backing and discarded, leaving an uncoated area (see Fig. 5.9). When the stencil has been ironed on to the screen mesh and the backing peeled off, open areas of mesh are left through which the colour can be printed.

As the design is literally cut by hand, a hard edge is produced. This makes the method an ideal one for geometric designs, or those with a definite outline. It is, therefore, not suitable for freely textured or 'splashy' designs, which are not possible to cut (see Fig. 5.10).

Experiments should be carried out before cutting an actual design, to discover the properties of Stenplex Amber (Profilm). A light-weight knife with a sharp pointed blade must be used – Scalpels are ideal, and many different types of blade are available for use with them. The pressure exerted by the knife should be just strong enough to score through to the backing.

Fig. 5.9 The 'knife-cut' stencil (Stenplex Amber).

Fig. 5.10 Hard-edged designs are most suitable for the cut stencil

Any cuts that actually cut *through* the backing show that the pressure on the blade is too great. The backing sheet must stay intact to support the remaining areas that have not been cut away. Any small cuts that overshoot the edges of shapes must be patched up later with small pieces of the film, as any cuts left unpatched will result in tiny lines appearing on the cloth during printing.

'Photographic' stencils

The versatility of screen printing is most clearly demonstrated by the use of the 'photographic' stencil. As the design is painted by hand on to drafting film, (e.g. Kodatrace; Permatrace) it is the most direct way of producing repeating spontaneous designs. There is virtually nothing painted on paper that cannot be repeated on cloth using this method. It is totally free, allowing for both soft and hard effects and, using special film and equipment, even controlled mechanical tones can be printed.

The term 'photographic' can be daunting, suggesting the use of specialised dark-room equipment. However, in reality the process can be as simple or as complicated as facilities allow. The term 'photographic', used in this context, applies to the technique of using light-sensitive liquid to coat the

Fig. 5.11 A group of one-colour prints produced using Kodatrace. Designs by second-year students of Berkshire College of Art and Design

screen. The design, on Kodatrace, is exposed on to a
sensitised screen using an ultraviolet light source.

The design is painted on the Kodatrace using special
opaque ink (if this is not available, a dense gouache, or even a
wax crayon can be used). Experiments with Kodatrace can
be very rewarding, and can yield results that can be used in
more conventional, or repeating, designs. Actual objects (if
they are flat and opaque enough) can be fixed to the Kodatrace,
forming part of a repeat if required. In fact, any suitably flat
object can be held directly in contact with the screen even
without the use of Kodatrace, and its image exposed on to the
screen (see Fig. 5.12).

Fig. 5.12 A variety of objec
exposed on to a screen dire
and printed

Any large areas or shapes on the Kodatrace can be filled in
with black paper (quicker than painting!) and hard outlines
and sharp angles formed with black adhesive tape. Letraset
and other types of adhesive transfers can be used on Kodatrace,
although experiments should be carried out to determine their
density, as, although they all look black, some are not opaque
enough for exposure purposes. Tonal effect transfers are
available, consisting of ranges of different-sized dots placed to
form tone (see Fig. 5.13). Again, experiments will determine
which dots are large enough to be compatible with the screen
mesh – not so small that they block with print-paste, yet dense
enough to expose in the first place. (Certain lines may also be too
fine, for the same reasons.) The most important principle to
remember is that whatever is to be exposed on to the screen
must be dense and opaque. It is a worthwhile precaution to
ensure, if actual objects are being used, that they are painted
black if there is doubt as to their opacity.

Fig. 5.13 A design using dot and tonal transfers. Design by Julia Lavis

Many textural effects can be produced using Kodatrace. They may be random, or can be cut to form a loose repeat. Wax crayons can be very successful when used on Kodatrace, and their effects can be heightened by leaving lots of little white areas between wax strokes. In this way the characteristics of the crayon are exaggerated, and reproduced exactly on cloth (see Fig. 5.14). Crayon *rubbings* can also be taken on Kodatrace, but wherever crayon is used in this way it must be dark and opaque – red or black, never blue.

Fig. 5.14 Crayon can be used on Kodatrace to create:
(a) A texture (design by Janie Martin); or

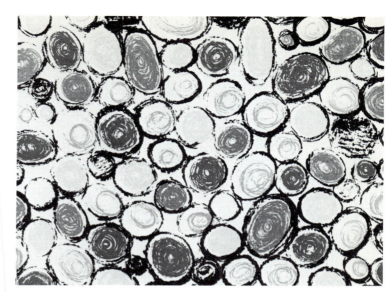

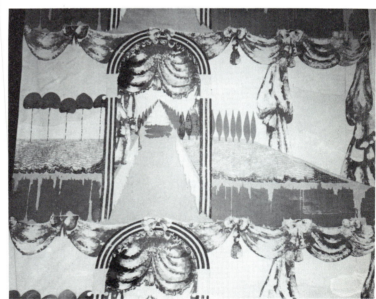

(b) To suggest tone.

Even using opaque fluid alone, many different textures can be created. It can be blown through a diffuser, and dabbed, sponged, or stippled on. It also can be painted on, and parts of it scraped off when dry (Fig. 5.15).

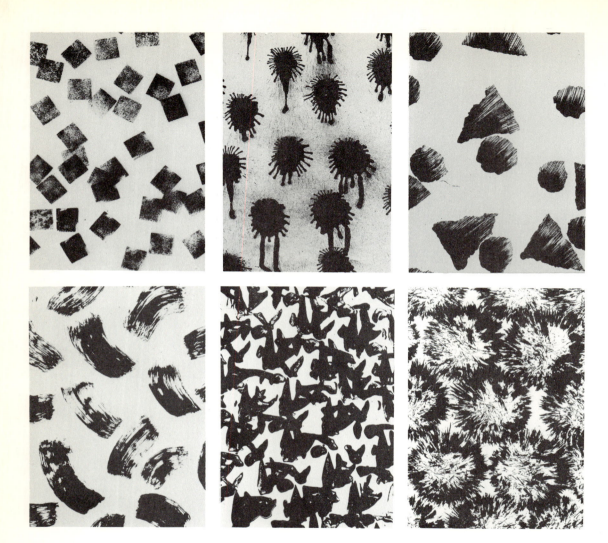

Fig. 5.15   Opaque can be applied in many different ways.
(a) Sponged on
(b) Blown through a diffuser
(c) Painted on and scraped off when dry
(d) Painted on semi-dry
(e) Stamped on with screwed paper
(f) Splodged on with a shaving-brush

The one thing that must on no account be attempted using opaque, is the creation of tone by diluting the opaque, i.e. by adding water and using it to fade the density so that the opaque becomes progressively lighter. Any lessening of opacity will allow the light through during exposure, and harden the screen coating, making printing impossible. Tonal effects can only be produced by the use of a photographic half-tone, 'Letraset' tone or other transfers which are opaque enough, or by a hand-drawn tone suggested by the placing of dots or small marks (see Fig. 5.16).

Fig. 5.16 Tone can be created
using 'photographic' exposure
methods.
(a) A mechanical half-tone print:
'Elephants at the Acropolis'

(b) A print produced using
'Letratone' on Kodatrace: Globes',
by Sarah Wheeler

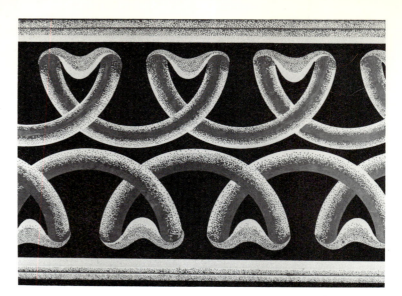

(c) Hand stippling on Kodatrace, using a ruling pen
(d) Free-hand stippling on Kodatrace. The white dots are made by leaving gaps in the opaque. Design by Vanessa Jones

PRINT-PASTES

Different dyestuffs are available for printing and dyeing various fabrics. Each type of dyestuff has an affinity with particular fabrics, and can be thickened to enable it to be printed. The mixing and fixing of some print-pastes can be complex and time-consuming, as fabrics require treatment after printing to fix the colour, and this may involve steaming or baking. Fortunately there is a type of print-paste which is easy to mix, easy to use, and easy to fix. These characteristics make 'pigment' print-pastes the obvious choice for use in schools and colleges, or anywhere where time and space are limited.

PIGMENTS

Pigment colours are supplied in a highly concentrated liquid form. They are extended by mixing with a binder, which appears white, but does not noticeably weaken the pure colour, except when it is used to form pale or pastel shades.

Different colours reach their full intensity when mixed with the binder in particular proportions, and care should be taken to follow suppliers' instructions with regard to recipes. Delicate colours and subtle tones can be made by mixing the concentrate (the colour) into the binder drop by drop. Binder should never be added to the colour, as pigment colours are so powerful that the tiniest drop is sufficient to colour a great deal of binder.

Pigments are transparent, which means that they can be overprinted to form intermediate colours. However, the results will rarely be as successful as when printing with dyes as the fact that pigments do not fully penetrate the fibre means that a surface build-up of colour will result from too much overprinting. This can give the fabric an unpleasant feel, and worse still, the colour may actually rub or peel off.

Pigments can be used to print on most fabrics, with the exception of wool. The matt effect that they have on shiny fabrics means that they can be used to change surface texture and appearance. This characteristic should be borne in mind when planning to print on pile fabrics, as pigments do not fully penetrate the pile, and create a stiff surface. Experiments should also be carried out to determine the effects of printing large areas of pigment on very fine fabrics.

Pigments are very versatile, as they can be printed, painted, and sprayed on to cloth. Black pigment is extremely dense and opaque, and is useful as a 'mask' or outline, up to which other colours can be painted. White pigment also has interesting characteristics. It is opaque, and should not be confused with the white binder, which is transparent. White pigment is mixed with the binder in the way that normal colours are, creating a matt white. This can produce very interesting and subtle effects when printed on to white backgrounds, especially shiny ones. It can be mixed with other colours (and the binder) to form opaque pastel shades which can be printed on to darker grounds. White pigment is the only means by which a light colour can be printed directly over a darker one without first discharging the background colour. (This can be useful when covering small blemishes!) White pigment does, however, give a solid feel to the fabric, and should not be used over a large area.

Pigment prints are fixed by the application of dry heat. Ideally, this should be carried out in a purpose-built baker. It should *never* be attempted in a domestic oven, especially a gas oven. Fortunately, it is possible to fix pigments by ironing. The iron must be set to as high a temperature as the fabric will stand, and each part of the print ironed slowly, several times, until the fumes and vapour arising from the pigment have gone.

FABRICS

In general, the best results will be achieved by working with natural fibres – cotton, linen, and silk. Care should be taken to buy fabrics that are specially prepared for printing; this means that they do not contain crease resists or finishes. It is wise to buy fabrics from a specialist supplier (see UK suppliers, p. 241), as almost all fabrics sold in the shops are 'finished' in some way.

Some fabrics are unsuitable for particular purposes. For example, a stretch fabric should not be used for a finely fitting repeat, and a plasticised fabric should not be used with any water-based print-pastes. As with all processes and media, experiment is worth while, and close attention to print suppliers'recipes is vital.

FROM DESIGN TO PRINT

For printing purposes, the amount of small repeats, or the size of the design that can be printed at one strike (one print of the screen) depends upon the size of the screen and the width of the fabric. Fabrics are sold in standard widths, dress fabrics generally being 90 and 115 cm, and furnishings, 122 and

Fig. 5.17 Ideally, screens should be considerably longer than the width of the cloth so that the printing area covers the cloth, leaving only a narrow unprinted area along each selvage

137 cm. Ideally, screens used for dress and furnishing should be considerably longer than the width of the fabric, so that the actual printing area covers the cloth (see Fig. 5.17).

Depending on whether the design or the screen is in existence first, the design can be produced to fit the screen, or the screen can be made to accommodate the design. If a small screen is used, it can still be positioned to repeat the design across the cloth, but for good registration and repeat, a full-size screen is necessary. Very small screens can be useful for printing samples, and for colour testing.

In Chapter 3 the procedure for putting a design into repeat was outlined. The design was cut through, and repositioned to repeat. It was ultimately housed in a rectangle that contained half shapes at one edge, and their corresponding other halves at another edge (see Fig. 3.21). If this design were to be put onto screens and printed in its present form, an obvious join-line would be visible where one half of a printed shape met its other half. This join-line might take the form of a white gap, or a dark overlap. It would occur across the fabric at regular intervals, and be very noticeable. Therefore, when a design is cut to repeat for printing, the cutting line must not be taken through the centre of shapes, but must follow their outlines. Figure 5.18 shows a design that has been cut on a straight line and Fig. 5.19 shows the same design cut to repeat for printing. In this form the

Fig. 5.18 A large design cut into repeat (see Ch. 3)

Fig. 5.19 The same design, cut to repeat for *printing*, avoids a visible join-line by being cut around shapes instead of through them.

design has some shapes that protrude in whole at one edge, and some that protrude at the other. Relevant gaps occur into which the protruding shapes fit. The line on which the design repeats is more or less invisible, as it follows the natural outlines of shapes. This is particularly important when dealing with grid-type designs (see Fig. 5.20)

CUTTING A DESIGN TO REPEAT FOR PRINTING

1. Draw an *accurate* rectangle (using a precision grid if possible). The rectangle forms a set of guidelines that are vitally important for registration. It may contain one full-width design, or a series of small repeated units. (see Fig. 5.21). To allow for the shapes that will eventually protrude at either side after cutting, the depth of the rectangle should be made approximately 23 cm narrower than the inside width of the screen (see Fig. 5.17) (The depth of the rectangle is the measurement across the narrowest edge. This allows extra space around the rectangle into which the the cut shapes can protrude without the depth of the design becoming too great for the screen. When using the small repeat networks, bear in

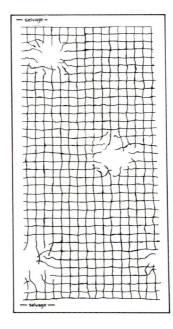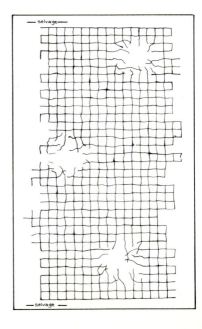

Fig. 5.20 Grids must be cut with particular care to avoid straight join-lines

mind the ways in which they can affect the overall size of the design. (see Fig. 5.21(b)).

2. Draw the design within the rectangle. If a non-repeating design is already in existence, it can be enclosed within a rectangle for purposes of repeat. (This need not restrict a free design, as the rectangle is eventually removed.)

If possible, the colour should be only suggested at this stage, as alterations will have to be made after cutting.

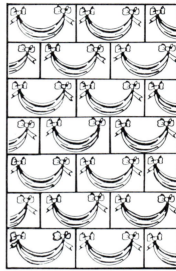

Fig. 5.21 (a) The original rectangle designed to fit the screen may contain one large or many small units
(B) Bear in mind how different repeat networks will affect the depth of the design

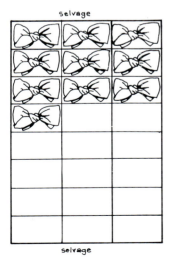
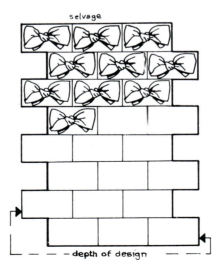
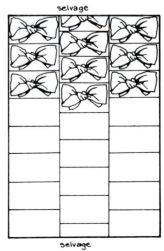

3. Cut through the design, as shown in Fig. 5.22, preferably using a sharp knife and not scissors. The background, if it is to be left unprinted, can be cut straight through. Shapes which are to be printed must be carefully cut around, separating them from each other. The cut line should not meander too far to one side or another, or else when the design is repositioned to repeat, it will be too wide for the screen.
4. When the design has been cut through, fix the left half firmly down (on a precision grid if possible).
5. Take the right half (B) and position it to the left of the left half, so that the horizontal rectangle lines are in line. Slide (B) along until the design fits, keeping the

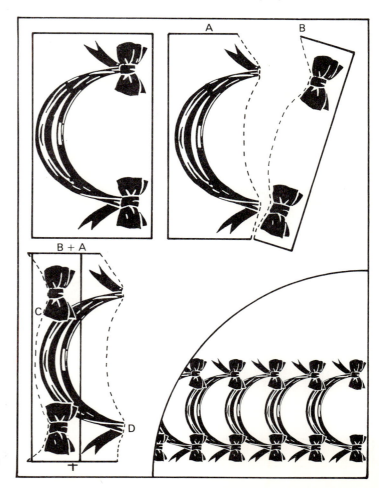

Fig. 5.22 Cutting the design to repeat for printing, and adding registration crosses

guidelines exactly in line, even though they may overlap. Check that the overall measurement from point C to point d (measuring horizontally, and not at an angle) is not too wide to fit the screen. If the design does prove to be too wide, the two halves can be moved to overlap, taking care to keep the registration guidelines (the rectangle) in perfect alignment.

6. Tape the two halves of the design together at intervals.

Where the new centre of the design occurs, shapes will probably clash. They may overlap, or may bear no relationship to each other. Any element can be altered throughout the design, *except* those whose outlines form the new outside edges. These must not be changed, as they are known to fit each other perfectly, and form the repeat.

7. Registration crosses should now be put in at the top and bottom of the design. They should be about 2 cm in size, and placed 0.5 cm outside the design. They must be parallel with each other and with the edge of the rectangle, and preferably traced through from the precision grid. They should be placed at about the centre between points C and D (see Fig. 5.22).

The registration crosses are of vital importance. They enable checks to be made at every stage, and they ensure that the design is placed squarely on the screen, and afterwards, on the cloth.

The accuracy of the repeat can be further checked by tracing if required (see Fig. 5.23.).

8. Tape a narrow length of good-quality tracing paper along one side of the design.

9. Trace the registration guidelines at the top and bottom of the design, extending them to the edges of the tracing paper.

10. Trace the design from top to bottom.

11. Move the tracing, and place it over the other side of the design, so that the registration guidelines are in line, and the two edges that were originally cut from each other fit together perfectly.

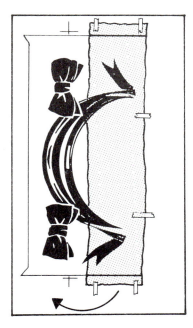

Fig. 5.23 Checking the repeat (if required) by tracing

TRANSFERRING THE DESIGN TO THE STENCIL

When the design is complete on paper, it is transferred to the stencil (Kodatrace or Stenplex Amber). If a close repeat has been designed, one very important point should be borne in mind: whichever method is used, it is vital that the design, and the stencil on top of it, are kept perfectly flat. The design should be firmly taped to a stable surface where it should stay until the stencils are complete. The design is taped down in the following way, to keep it as flat as possible. This might seem a trivial procedure but it is vital to keep the design flat.

1. Tape along one side of the design, using small pieces of tape placed about 8 cm apart. Smooth the paper as you tape it.
2. Pushing the design flat across to the other side, tape it in the same way.
3. Tape the third and fourth edges, continually smoothing the design. Any protruding cut shapes should be carefully treated so that they do not move or bend.
   Do not simply tape the design down using one long piece of tape at each edge, as it will undoubtedly buckle. Good registration is at stake!
4. Tape, in the same way, the Kodatrace or Stenplex Amber over the design (this is not cut into a shape but is simply rectangular). It should be at least 8 cm larger than the design. Cut out (or paint black, as appropriate) all the areas that are to be printed in the same colour. Shapes must be made slightly larger on the stencils, to give an overlap of at least 1 mm. This prevents white gaps occurring during printing.

Be sure to put in the registration crosses. The original guidelines formed by the rectangle now serve naturally as the edges of the design. They are not needed on the stencil except where they form an edge to the design. Their place has been taken, for purposes of registration, by two pencilled lines, (marked 'A') and placed as shown in Fig. 5.24. They should be placed in line with the registration crosses, and be about 5 cm in length.

Fig. 5.24 Pencilled lines drawn on the stencil are a further registration guide

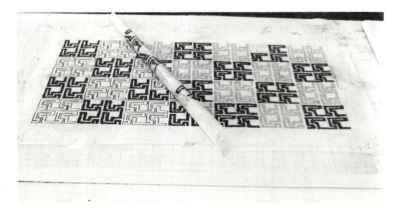

Fig. 5.25 Stencils should be worked on top of one another, and kept in place until the work is complete

5. Place successive stencils on top of the design and each other; one stencil for each colour. They can be added so long as the design remains clearly visible (Fig. 5.25).

Place the registration crosses on each stencil, and mark in the pencilled guidelines. (You should be able to draw with pencil on Stenplex Amber, although it is preferable to cut the registration crosses in this case.)

When the stencils are complete, remove them from the design. Cut stencils are ready to be fixed to the screen (see ironing procedure below).

Kodatrace must be checked against the light for patchy areas.

Checking the Kodatrace

It might be a nasty shock, on viewing the Kodatrace against the light, to find that some black-painted areas are not as dense as they appeared to be. Many of the black areas will need some 'touching up'. Some may show greasy patches over which the opaque has not settled, some may have 'pinholes', and some may be streaky. These faults can be quickly remedied by retouching the Kodatrace against the light (fixed to a window, or, preferably, a light box). Greasy patches, which are easily recognised at the time of painting, can be removed by rubbing the Kodatrace with liquid soap or methylated spirits prior to, or during painting.

TRANSFERRING THE STENCIL TO THE SCREEN

The image on Kodatrace is transferred to the screen 'photographically' (see p. 109). Stenplex Amber is attached to the screen by ironing.

Before ironing the Stenplex Amber to the screen, the screen should be degreased by washing with a degreasing agent.

Stenplex Amber ironing procedure

1. If a repeating design is being used, draw a line on the screen mesh at the top. The line should be approximately 10 cm away from the inside edge of the frame to allow space for a dye-well.
2. A flat ironing surface should be prepared, consisting of a

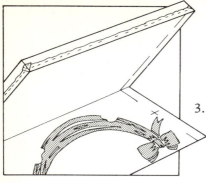

Fig.5.26   Positioning the Stenplex Amber on the screen

thick bed of newspapers. Lay the Stenplex Amber *shiny side up* on the newspapers, so that the cross and the pencil registration lines at the top of the stenplex coincide with the line drawn on the screen mesh (see Fig. 5.26). An even space should also be left at either side of the design. Each screen used with the design must have the line drawn on it in the same place.

3. Lay a piece of clean, greaseproof paper inside the screen, and iron it gently with a warm iron. The shellac coating of the Stenplex Amber will become darker as it melts into the screen mesh, and the backing sheet can eventually be slowly peeled off. Should a piece of backing be pulled off too soon, before the coating has properly adhered to the screen, the coating can be reironed, provided a loose piece of the backing sheet is placed under the part to be ironed – otherwise the coating will stick to the table.

4. The screen must now be edged with gumstrip (see Fig. 5.6). The gumstrip must be placed in such a way that any areas of open mesh left between the stencil and the frame are covered.

This type of screen is water soluble, and must be varnished to make it long-lasting. It is possible to use an unvarnished screen if it is only washed once, and very gently. Generally speaking, the screen should be varnished if it is intended either to be used for a long run, or to be washed between prints.

Varnishing

Two types of varnish are used to make the screen waterproof, each with its relevant solvent – paper varnish and turpentine, and knotting and methylated spirits. The procedure is as follows.

1. Place the screen face side upwards (i.e. the side which has the mesh on it). Support the corners of the screen (e.g. across two tables, or on large blocks of wood) so that free access is available to reach under the screen.

2. Take the paper varnish, and brush it over the uppermost side of the screen. Simply cover the screen with varnish, do not drench it.

3. The open areas of mesh are now clogged with varnish. They can be cleared, without removing the varnish from the actual stencil, by wiping the screen mesh *underneath*, using rags soaked with turpentine. Change the rags frequently, rubbing the underside of the mesh with a circular

motion, until the exposed areas of mesh are completely clear. This leaves the solid areas on the face side of the screen covered in varnish. (The screen should not have been so freely covered with varnish that it continues to run and reblock the mesh.)

4. Leave the screen supported, and allow it to dry (preferably overnight).

5. Turn the screen over, and repeat the above process, using knotting and methylated spirits. Any varnish for which methylated spirits is the solvent can be used.

   Rags dampened with methylated spirits may safely be rubbed over the paper-varnished side of the screen without danger of removing the varnish. The rags should be continually changed to ensure that only clean solvent reaches the mesh, as any blocked patches will be permanent.

6. Leave the screen to dry.

This method results in a long-lasting and durable screen, but it is more or less permanent, and a great deal of work would be involved to prepare it for use with another design.

COATING AND EXPOSING PHOTOGRAPHIC SCREENS

The coating used for photographic screens is mixed from two components: one a light-sensitive liquid, the other a polyvinyl emulsion. The coating, when dry, is hardened by exposure to ultraviolet light. Any areas of the coated screen that are protected from the light remain soft, and can be washed out. The function of the dark shapes painted on the Kodatrace is to protect parts of the screen from the light. When the screen is washed after exposure the areas of coating that were protected from the light wash out, leaving clear areas of uncoated mesh in the shape of the design that was held in contact with the screen.

Only screens that are tightly and evenly stretched are suitable for photographic exposure, as an even layer of emulsion cannot be applied to sagging or loose screens.

As the screen-coating emulsion is light sensitive, the screen must be coated in a dark-room, or if a dark-room is not available, in *very dim diffuse light*. Any room can be darkened by blacking out the windows, but the light-sensitive liquid itself must always be stored in total darkness.

The screen must stand upright while being coated, so a clear space of wall should be set aside in the dark-room for this purpose.

A special trough is used to coat the screen (see UK suppliers, p. 240). Choose a trough that is slightly shorter than the inside width of the screen, and can therefore be moved freely up and down the screen.

Mix the coating liquid carefully according to manufacturers' recipes. It is important to leave it to stand for some time, so check instructions.

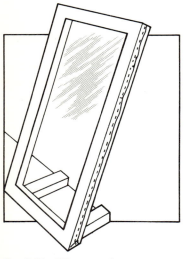

Fig. 5.27 When coating a screen, blocks of wood are used to hold the screen at the correct angle away from the wall

Screen coating procedure

1. Lean the screen against the wall in the dark-room, face side outwards, and place blocks of wood between the screen and the wall in the position shown in Fig. 5.27. These pieces of wood hold the screen firmly away from the wall at the bottom, and prevent is slipping back while it is being coated.
   Half fill the trough, and hold it at the base of the screen against the mesh.
2. Tilt the trough until the fluid touches the mesh, and exerting an even pressure, draw it up the mesh, just stopping short of the screen frame at the top. The mesh must be evenly coated, and must not show any runs or blobs.
3. Turn the screen over, and repeat the procedure on the inside.
4. Turn the screen back to its original position, and using an empty trough, firmly draw off the excess coating, using the same movement that was used to coat the screen.
5. Repeat the procedure on the other side.
6. Leave the screen resting horizontally in a dark place, and leave it until it is dry – preferably overnight. If time is short, the screen can be dried more quickly using a cold fan. A high temperature must never be used to dry screens.

Screen exposure procedure

All the procedures set out below must be carried out in a dark-room.

If more than one Kodatrace is being used in a design, it is important that each one be placed in exactly the same position on each screen. It is for this purpose that the registration crosses and pencil guidelines have been drawn on the drafting film. A corresponding pencil line must now be drawn on to the screen mesh.

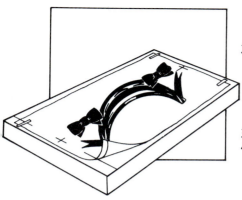

Fig. 5.28 Aligning the pencil lines on the Kodatrace with those on the screen

1. Rest the screen face up, and at one end, 10 cm away from the inside edge of the frame and draw a line across the mesh. If the screen already has bolt holes drilled into one end, use this end.
2. Lay the Kodatrace on top of the screen *face down*, with the painted areas in contact with the mesh, so that there is an equal gap at either side of it. Align the nearest cross and pencilled guidelines on the Kodatrace with the line on the screen mesh. Tape the Kodatrace to the screen at each corner (see Fig. 5.28).
3. Expose the screen.
4. When the screen has been exposed, remove the Kodatrace, and take the screen quickly to the wash-off trough. The entire screen will continue to expose now that it is in the light, so it should be quickly sprayed with cool water on both sides. It must not be rubbed, as the coating is in a delicate condition at this stage. Continue to spray on the face side until the design appears.

   All areas of the screen that were protected from the light will wash out.
5. When the screen has been thoroughly washed, the design will be seen on it as clear areas of mesh.

   Lay the screen face down on a bed of newspaper. Blot, but do not rub it. Screens must never be rubbed when damp as small particles of lint flake off cloth and newspaper, and block the mesh.
6. Lay the screen face up in the light until it is totally dry. Should the exposure have been unsuccessful the screen can be bleached and used again. (It can also be bleached when it is finished with, see pp. 90, 119).
7. When the screen is completely dry, hold or stand it against the light, and check it for small pinholes or breaks in the coating. These must be blocked with the screen coating liquid. If whole sections of pinholes occur, the coating can be 'squeegeed' on using a small piece of card as a squeegee. (A small amount of screen coating can safely be taken into the light for this purpose.)

Gumstripping

The join between the edge of the screen frame and the mesh must now be covered with brown-paper tape (gumstrip). Any open areas of mesh between the edges of the coating and the frame must also be gumstripped (see Fig. 5.6). In the case of photographic screens the coating is bleached off when the screen is finished with. Therefore it is a semi-permanent stencil and the gumstrip, which must also be removed later, should not be varnished.

REGISTRATION OF SCREENS

When a screen is being printed it is difficult to see through the mesh which becomes stained with print-paste, and this means that screens cannot be accurately registered by eye.

The registration crosses which have been put onto the screen along with the design are part of a process by which the screen can be accurately set up to register in the same place on every 'strike'. The registration bar and stops are another part of this process.

Print tables that have no registration bar can be used for loosely repeating designs or completely random ones. For designs that form a close repeat, or incorporate several different screens, a purpose-built print table with a bar should be used.

Registering screens on a purpose-built print table, using wooden screens

For this procedure (see below) a precision grid is used. If a design which has a very loosely fitting repeat is being registered, a large sheet of graph paper could be used. However, it should be borne in mind that a precision grid is exactly that – precise – and there is no real substitute for precise and accurate instruments. Precision grids are expensive, but necessary for good screen registration.

Procedure

1. Drill two holes at the top end of the screen in the positions marked A and B in Fig. 5.29. The top is the end at which the pencil line has been drawn.

    The holes should be placed about 8 cm in from each corner, and drilled to take heavy 7 cm screws (coach screws would be ideal). Screw them in until about 1 cm of thread is showing.

2. Lay a precision grid on the print table, and place the screen in the centre face down on the grid, screws towards the bar. Set the cross at the top end of the screen (nearest you) about 5 mm above the first major line on the grid.

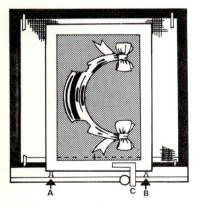

Fig. 5.29 Registering screens on a purpose-built print table. Note the position of the screws (A and & B) resting on the bar, and the bracket (C) against the stop.

3. Take hold of the edge of the grid, and gently draw it, with the screen still on it, towards the bar, until the screws just touch the bar. Remove the screen, leaving the grid exactly in position.

It will help at this stage if an actual cross has been marked in the centre of the relevant grid line. This cross will eventually align with the cross on the screen.

4. Measure the distance from the bar to the cross on the grid. Adjust the grid so that it is exactly parallel to the bar. Tape it to the table.

5. Take the Kodatrace that matches the screen, and lay it on the grid face up. Align the cross and the pencilled guidelines on the Kodatrace with the relevant cross and grid line. Tape the Kodatrace firmly to the grid.

6. Laying the screen on top of the Kodatrace, gently adjust the screws until the design on the screen exactly fits the design on the Kodatrace, and both the screws touch the bar. The registration crosses on the screen should align with those on the Kodatrace.

The screws might seem to be different lengths at this stage, but they serve simply to set the *design* square to the bar, not necessarily the screen.

7. Lay a flat right-angle bracket on the screen frame in the position marked C in Fig. 5.29. Screw it to the frame.

8. Set a stop on the bar against the inside of the bracket, and lock it into position.

9. Now lift the screen, and move it down the table until it sits beside the Kodatrace. Looking through the screen mesh, move the screen carefully until the repeat joins up (see Fig. 5.30). The screws must not leave the bar, neither may they be adjusted again, even if the repeat does not fit.

10. When the screen forms the repeat, set a second stop to fit the bracket. Be sure to set it at the same side of the bracket as before.

The distance between the two stops is the *depth of repeat*. The depth of repeat must be measured from the same side of one stop to the same side of the next stop (see Fig. 5.30). Both the depth of repeat and the distance at which the fabric is to be placed from the bar should be written on the screen frame for reference. The fabric must be placed parallel to the bar at a distance that ensures that the design is printed centrally.

11. Lock a series of stops along the bar, set to this exact measurement.

It is a good idea to get someone to check your stops, as the slightest deviation from the measurement can cause a mis-registration along the repeat join. The screen bracket

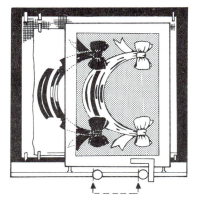

Fig. 5.30 Moving the screen along the table to make the repeat join up

rests against a stop at each repeat, ensuring that the design is in exactly the same position every time.

Subsequent screens are registered on the master Kodatrace, although more Kodatraces can be added to it if necessary. The bracket on each screen must rest against the same side of the stop.

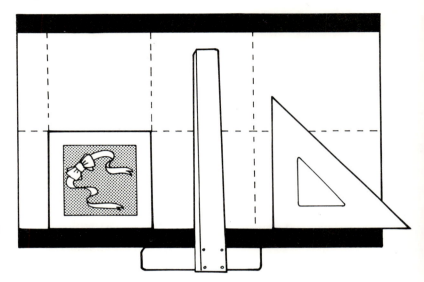

Fig. 5.31 Registering a screen on a table that has no registration rail

Registration of screens without a registration bar

Registering screens on a table that has no registration bar is less straightforward, and two points should be borne in mind:

1. It is unwise to attempt to register a very close-fitting design or fine repeat using a home-made print table.
2. Screens that are old, uneven, and rough are also unsuitable for use with this method. Screens must be smooth and well finished as it is important that they fit into accurately drawn guidelines on the cloth.

The procedure for registration is as follows. (see Fig. 5.31).

1. Lay the screen on the table about 6 cm away from the table edge.
2. Mark the position of the nearest edge of the screen on the table. Remove the screen.
3. Draw a parallel line along the table at this distance from the edge.

4. Lay the fabric along this line. (Once experience is gained the position of the actual *print* on the fabric can be gauged by eye and the placing of the fabric adjusted accordingly.)
5. Fix the fabric to the table (see pages 84–5).
6. Lay the screen on the cloth so that the edge of the screen frame rests against the edge of the fabric.
7. Using tailor's chalk, mark the position of the corners of the screen on the fabric.
8. Using either (a) a very large set square resting against the edge of the cloth, or (b) a large T-square pressed against the edge of the table, draw two parallel chalk lines *across* the fabric, using the corner marks as guide-points.
9. Now draw a line *along* the fabric to join and continue the two points that mark the position of the far corners of the screen. (If a large screen is being used this far line will not be necessary.)

These grid lines form a framework within which the screen fits on each repeat. If a very small screen is being used the dimensions of the screen can be used to add further guidelines across the cloth.

The screen can also be deliberately and consistently positioned off register if required by adding more guidelines – provided that track is kept of which guidelines are which!

Other screens which are part of the design can also be registered within the same guidelines, provided that the stencils have been placed in the same position on each screen. (Use registration crosses and pencil guidelines.)

Registering interlocking designs without a registration bar

Designs which incorporate loosely interlocking repeats – as opposed to motif, or tile-type designs – can be registered on a print table that does not have a bar, although obviously the procedure is slightly more complicated than that just outlined.

The registration is carried out on waste cloth which is fixed to the table in the normal way. A supply of newsprint should be kept to hand for blotting.

The procedure is as set out below.

Follow the previously outlined procedure to no. 6.

7. Draw a line, at a right angle to the selvage, across the cloth, at the far left-hand side. Place the screen against this line, the nearest edge resting along the edge of the fabric (see Fig. 5.32(a)).

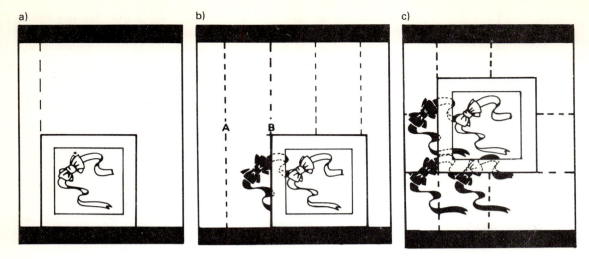

a)   b)   c)

Fig. 5.32 Registering an
interlocking repeat on a table that
has no rail.

8. Print the screen, using a pale/medium colour. Wash and dry the screen. (p. 118) (For printing procedure see below.)

9. When the screen is dry, place it back over the printed image. Move the screen slowly along the fabric, looking through the mesh until the printed image and the image on the screen interlock. The shapes that protrude on one side of the screen will fit into gaps left at the other side on the printed image.

10. Leaving the screen in position, take the measurements between points A and B. Make a mark on the cloth at point B (see Fig. 5.32(b)).

11. Remove the screen. Draw a line across the cloth using point B as a guidepoint. This second line should be exactly parallel with the first.

12. Draw further lines across the cloth at this distance apart. These lines are the depth of the repeat, and form a framework within which the screen fits.

   There are now several guidelines that determine the position of the screen on the cloth. One is the line formed by the selvage, and the others are those that cross the cloth at right angles to the selvage. The left-hand side of the screen, and the edge that rests along the selvage touch these guidelines on each repeat. The right-hand side may or may not rest against a line, but in any event is not used for registration in this case, as the size of the repeat framework has been reduced due to the fact that the screen has been lapped over the print on each repeat to make the design interlock.

13. When the guidelines have been drawn up, the screen can

be printed a second time to interlock with the first print, checking that the repeat does actually fit. On subsequent repeats it will not be necessary to look through the mesh to check the repeat; the screen is simply placed within the lines drawn on the cloth.

14. The screen can be used to form a repeat at top and bottom, as well as side to side, by following the same procedure. It would be wise in this case to print all the sideways-fitting repeats first, as too many registration grid lines on the cloth can be confusing (See Fig. 5.32(c)).

15. When you are certain that the measurements of the grid are accurate, remove the test print cloth, replace it with the cloth that is to be printed, and transfer the grid measurements to the new piece of cloth.

PRINTING

When printing, a helper can be invaluable. While it is possible to print a small screen single-handed, when printing a large screen two printers are required, both of whom should use the same printing pressure. (As the squeegee is passed from one to another half-way across the screen, an uneven pressure on the squeegee produces an uneven print.)

Printing Procedure

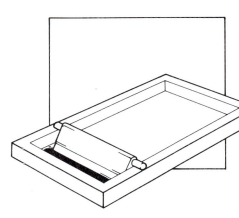

Fig. 5.33 The squeegee acts as a barrier between the print-paste and the design, prior to printing

1. Place the squeegee upright in the screen to form a dye-well. (see Fig. 5.33). Lean it away from you; the handles or screws that project from it will support it by resting against the screen frame.

2. Fill the dye-well with print-paste. The squeegee will act as a barrier between the print-paste and the edge of the design (see Fig. 5.33). If you do not have a helper, place heavy weights on the corners of the screen frame.

3. Now place the squeegee behind the print-paste. Tilt it at a slight angle away from you, and push it across the screen, maintaining a firm but medium pressure.

The cloth and the type of design determine how often the screen should be printed. For most medium-weight fabrics twice is enough. If unsure, it is wise to test print the design first on a spare piece of cloth.

When printing a length of fabric, care should be taken to prevent the screen resting on a wet print. If this should occur the screen will pick up an after-image which will be transferred to the cloth at the next repeat. To avoid this occurrence, alternate repeats are printed (see Fig. 5.34). The first print is then moderately dry by the time the last one has been printed. Those in between can then be printed without the danger that an impression from a damp print will be picked up.

If a short length is being printed, a fan heater set to 'warm' can be used to dry the prints. However, hot air should not be directed at the screen as it will become blocked if exposed to heat.

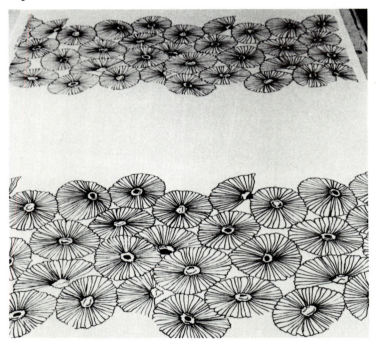

Fig. 5.34 Alternate repeats are printed to avoid wet colour pick-up

WASHING SCREENS

1. Remove excess print-paste from the screen with a flexible spatula.
2. Place the screen upright in the wash-off trough, face side away from you.
3. Soak both sides, and use a hose to squirt off remaining print-paste. The pigment will leave a slight stain on the mesh. This should be removed with a sponge dipped in soap powder. Wipe the screen on both sides with the sponge, and rinse.

The screen should be washed directly the print is finished, as print-paste which dries very quickly, will clog the screen. Screens incorporating fine lines, dots, or small areas of open mesh are particularly prone to blocking.

STRIPPING THE STENCIL FROM PHOTOGRAPHIC SCREENS

Special screen-clearing fluids can be used to strip photo-screens. However, a soaking in bleach and water will suffice to remove some of the more commonly used coatings such as 'Proset'.

A mixture of approximately 25 per cent bleach to 75 per cent water should be used, depending upon the strength of the bleach. The task of clearing screens is made easier by the use of a screen-blasting machine which is used after the screen has been soaked in bleach. If a screen blaster is not available, water should be squirted on to the screen under pressure from an ordinary hose. (Acetone can be rubbed over the screen when it is dry to remove dried smears of pigment.)

Small stubborn blockages can be removed with a high-pressure needle-jet gun (see Fig. 5.35). (The needle jet of water can also be used to blast a fine line through the screen coating at any stage to produce spontaneous shapes which can then be repeated during printing.)

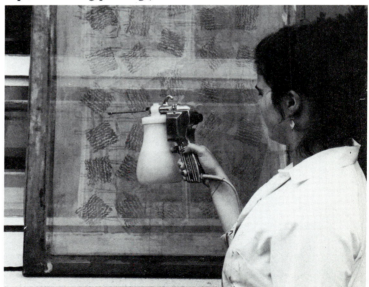

Fig. 5.35 The needle-jet gun

FURTHER RESISTS, STENCILS, AND TECHNIQUES FOR USE WITH THE SCREEN

Paper pick-up   Blottings
Direct stencils   Powder resist
Direct blockout   Marbling
Grease resist   Colour grading/shading
Screen rubbings   Wet on wet

Paper Pick-up: the simplest stencil

One sheet of newspaper (or preferably white newsprint) is enough to resist print-paste and act as a stencil. It can be used to produce a positive image, in which a shape is cut out of a sheet of paper and printed through, or a negative, in which case a shape is cut out and printed around. The first results in a coloured shape, the second in a coloured background.

To form a stencil, the sheet of paper is cut or torn, and placed underneath the screen. It should not be taped, either to the screen, or the print table. If a sheet of newsprint is to be used as a positive stencil it should be larger than the screen, so that the edges project beyond the screen and can be lifted and picked up with the screen. If a moderately sized motif is being used to print *around*, the print paste passing over it will

Fig. 5.36 'Paper pick-up' print with hand-painted dots

hold it to the screen, and it will automatically lift up with the screen.

Paper pick-up stencils can be used several times, although they do have a tendency to buckle when wet. If the stencil distorts badly, or looks extremely wet, it should be abandoned.

Special low-tack adhesive paper is available which can be used as a stencil. As it is ironed into position on the cloth it is easier to hold in place than loose newsprint, and makes a slightly more permanent stencil which is easily pulled off the cloth when the print is complete (see heat fix paper listed under UK suppliers, p. 241).

Paper Masking

Newsprint can also be used in conjunction with screens that already have a permanent design on them.

By masking, designs of several colours can be produced from the same screen. To achieve this, newsprint can be used in one of two ways:

a) b)

c) d)

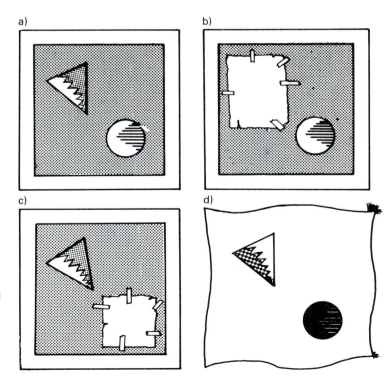

Fig. 5.37 Two colours printed from one screen.
(a) The original screen
(b) The first shape is masked, and the screen printed
(c) The first shape is uncovered, the second masked, and the screen printed again in a different colour
(d) The final print

1. Parts of the design on the screen can be covered with newsprint on the face side, the newsprint being held on with masking tape. The screen is then printed twice – the first time with selected shapes covered, and the second time with them uncovered. This will produce a partial overprint, as one area is printed twice.
2. Two completely separate colours can be printed from the same screen without an overprint if shapes that are masked on the first print are uncovered on the second, and vice versa (see Figs. 5.37 and 5.38).

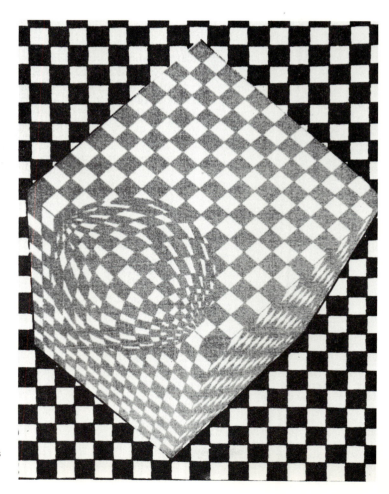

Fig. 5.38 A design in two colours printed from one screen, in the same way as Fig 5.37

Fig. 5.39 Newsprint and tape used to mask parts of a print.
(a) Some areas of the print are covered to conserve them during future printing

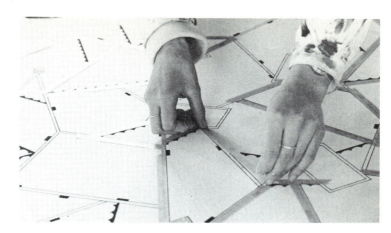

(b) A second screen is then printed over the whole area, and later the newsprint and tape are removed

(c) This leaves the second print on the areas of cloth that were not masked.

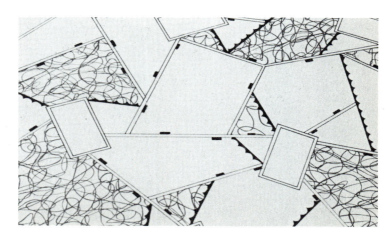

Parts of the design *on the cloth* can be masked with newsprint. The newsprint will conserve all the areas that it covers. (see Fig. 5.39). With this method the whole screen is printed first. Then selected areas on the cloth that are not being reprinted, are covered with newsprint and masking tape (Fig. 5.39(a)). A second screen is then used. The second screen may be blank, or may have a pattern on it (such as that used in Fig. 5.39). The screen is used to print over the whole area – the clear cloth and the newsprint that covers it.

When the newsprint and tape are removed, the pattern produced by the second screen will remain on the cloth only.

Masking tape is an extremely good masking medium, as its name implies. It can be stuck to the cloth or to the screen. If stuck to the cloth it can be left in position and printed over many times, provided that it is blotted each time. However, it must not be left overnight, or for any length of time as it becomes increasingly difficult to remove. (For use of masking tape as a stencil see Fig. 9.19.)

Direct stencils

Actual objects can be used as 'direct stencils', provided that they are thin enough to enable good contact to be maintained

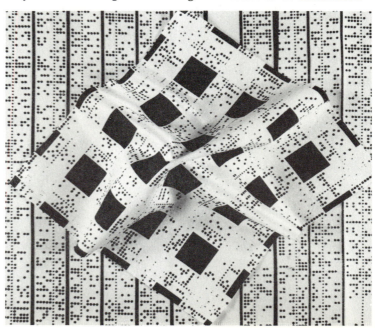

Fig. 5.40 Objects used as direct stencils (placed under the screen (a) Computer print-out tape

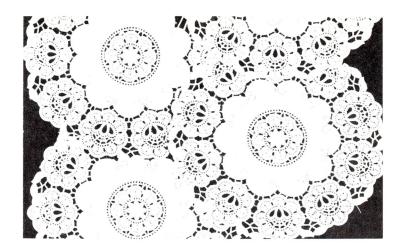

(b) Paper doillies

(c) Ferns

between the screen mesh and the print table.

As has been outlined previously (p. 93), objects can be fixed to drafting film and exposed on to the screen. This produces a positive image in which the object is printed as it appears on the drafting film, the background remaining uncoloured. If the object is placed directly under the screen at the time of printing, it produces a 'negative' image, or one in which the shape of the object appears blank, and the background is printed. Therefore, large evenly shaped objects will not produce such an interesting shape as those which are perforated in some way, or which have an uneven edge. A wide variety of objects can be used as direct stencils. (see Fig. 5.40).

Fig. 5.41 (a) Torn flat seed-pods placed under a blank screen and printed

(b) The same objects placed under a screen that already contains a pattern (the grid)

If the objects used are thin or fine enough, the print-paste will hold them on to the screen mesh when the screen is lifted, and they can be used to form a repeat when the screen is replaced. Alternatively, the objects can be blotted and dried, and used again, either as an overprint with parts cut out of them, or simply in misregister to form an overprint.

If the background around the objects has been printed in a very dark colour, (preferably black) further colour can be added to the print (e.g. by hand painting) without the need to mask the image.

Fig. 5.42 Design produced with torn paper where the shapes appear to be behind the grid, and not on the same level

The objects can also be used in conjunction with a screen carrying a more permanent stencil. They are placed under the screen in the normal way, but appear to be fragmented by the stencil (see Fig. 5.41(b)).

If a rigidly shaped pattern such as the grid seen in Fig. 5.42 is used the objects can be made to appear to be behind the grid by printing the grid first. The printed grid is then masked off on the cloth, the objects are placed over it, and colour printed through a blank screen. The objects protect the cloth from the print-paste, and the masking tape protects the printed grid from the objects and the print-paste. (see Fig. 5.42).

Direct blockout

Direct blockout stencils are so called because the screen mesh is blocked with a filler (usually varnish), forming a direct and permanent stencil. All the shapes that are not to be printed are blocked out on the screen. A design can be drawn onto the screen first, or the varnish can be painted on directly and spontaneously (see Fig. 5.43). Proceed as follows.

1. Gumstrip the screen. (Fig. 5.6).
2. On the face side of the screen, paint out with varnish all the parts that are not to be printed. The varnish must not be applied so thickly that it runs.
   Designs of more than one colour can be produced by reblocking and reprinting.

Printing more than one colour by overprint, using direct blockout

1. Decide which areas are to be printed first. If large areas of mesh are left open at this stage it will leave scope for reblocking later, which will allow more colours to be overprinted.
2. Varnish out on the screen all parts that are not to print.

Fig. 5.43 A direct blockout print

3. Print the first colour. Choose a medium to pale colour, as it acts as a base on top of which other colours are printed.
4. Wash the screen, blot, and dry it.
5. As the palest colour has already been printed, the pigment will not have stained the screen mesh so much that it cannot be seen through. Lay the screen back on to the print, on or off register as required, and mark on the mesh which parts of the original print you wish to keep in the existing colour. Remove the screen and block out more areas of mesh. Print-paste cannot penetrate any part of the screen that is coated with varnish, and areas of the first print are retained in this way.
6. When the varnish is dry, reprint the screen in a darker or stronger colour. The screen can be reblocked and reprinted several times. Colours must be chosen carefully to obtain the required effect and to avoid the possibility of peeling that can occur if too many layers of pigments are used.

A stripping agent can be painted on to the mesh to remove parts of the coating if a very free design is being produced. In theory the entire coating could be removed with a varnish stripper, and the screen used again, but in practice this procedure is time-consuming and laborious.

Grease resist

There are several different ways of using grease as a resist. With some methods the grease is applied directly to the cloth (e.g. with a candle or melted wax) with others it is applied to the screen mesh. Alternatively, the grease can act as a temporary blockout to a more permanent resist, i.e. a varnish.

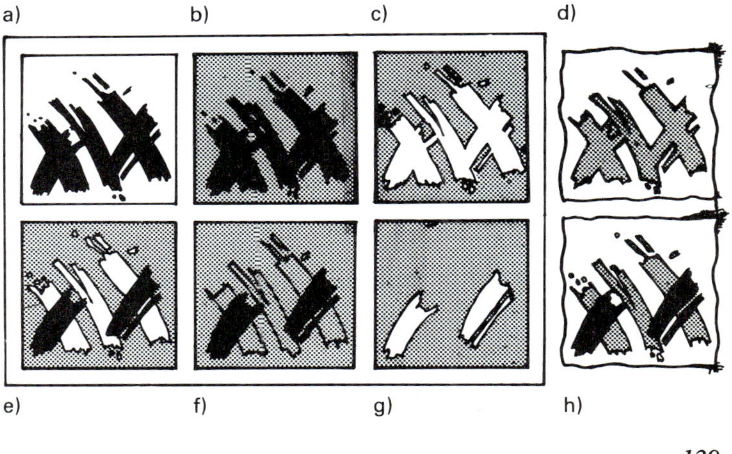

a) b) c) d)

e) f) g) h)

Fig. 5.44 The grease-resist procedure.
(a) The 'tusched' design
(b) The knotting is applied
(c) The tusche is removed
(d) The first print
(e) More tusche is applied to the screen
(f) The screen is recoated
(g) The tusche is removed
(h) The final two-colour print

This method is generally called 'grease resist', and is not as complicated as it sounds. It is easy to envisage the final results with grease resist, as it is the image to be printed that is originally blocked out on the screen. This approach is more spontanneous than direct blockout, as with grease resist it is not necessary laboriously to paint out whole areas of background around shapes.

The grease which is generally used as a liquid blockout in this instance (although any greasy media can be used) is tusche, which is a lithographic ink. A lithographic crayon, or a candle are useful for producing textured areas. The procedure is as follows (see Fig. 5.44).

1. Gumstrip the edges of the screen frame.
2. Paint the design on the screen with the tusche exactly as it is to be printed. (If a texture is being produced using a wax crayon or a candle, the wax must be well rubbed into the mesh.)
3. Wait for the tusche to dry. When it is dry, completely cover the screen mesh and gumstrip with knotting (or varnish). Wipe any large areas of varnish off the tusche with a solvent-dampened rag.
4. When the knotting is dry, apply another coat if neccessary. Leave the screen to dry again for several hours.
5. When the knotting is dry, hold the screen under warm running water to loosen the tusche. Blot the screen and dry it. Rub the tusched areas with rags soaked in white spirit. The tusche will wipe away, leaving the original painted areas clear.

After printing, further areas can be reblocked in the same way, and overprinted with different colours. It should be noted, however, that the drying time of the knotting means that the printed fabric must remain on the table for long periods of time.

Other resists to varnish

Tusche, in its original form, i.e. water-based, is becoming increasingly difficult to obtain. Most tusche today is spirit or vinyl based, and so does not wash out in water. Obviously, any spirit used to dissolve it on a screen mesh would also attack the varnish that covered it.

If it proves very difficult to obtain water-soluble tusche, experiments could be carried out with water-based gums. So-called 'drawing gums' which are a rubber solution that acts as a resist, are available in France but very difficult, as yet, to obtain in Britain. However, various commercial water-based gums may be found to be suitable for temporary screen filling.

One such gum is marketed by Marler in Britain under the name 'Marlerflex transfer gum 221' (see UK supplies, p. 241). It is water soluble, and can be used as a resist to varnish. It can be hosed and rubbed out of the screen mesh with warm water.

When using gum and varnish the procedure listed above for grease resist should be followed, substituting the gum for the tusche. Wherever possible, surplus varnish should be wiped off the gummed areas to make it easier to hose the gum away, as the process will be more difficult if quantities of varnish have hardened on top of the gum.

Rubbing and blotting

Rubbings can be used in printing in a variety of ways

1. They can be taken directly on to the screen mesh to form a resist – either to a more permanent screen coating or simply to the print-paste (see Fig. 5.45).
2. They can also be taken on to Kodatrace, using a dark wax crayon, and exposed onto a screen photographically.
3. Rubbings can be made directly onto cloth using fabric crayons (see Ch. 9, p. 218 and Fig. 9.4).

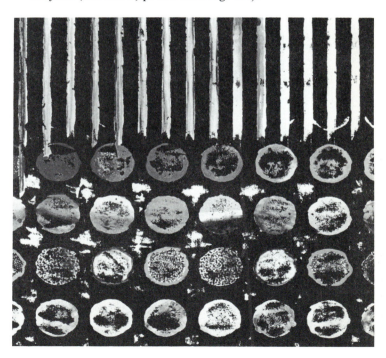

Fig. 5.45 A rubbing taken directly on to a socreen using a candle; printed, and then hand coloured.

4. They can also be taken in the form of a transfer or 'print-off' from a damp print to a dry piece of paper. This technique is listed under 'blotting'.

Rubbings are easily taken on to the screen mesh. The screen is simply placed face down on a textured surface, and the rubbing taken in the normal way, using the screen mesh in place of paper.

The screen then can be used in many different ways. If simply printed in one colour it leaves areas of the cloth blank that can later be coloured by hand. It can also be deliberately placed out of register with a second colour, giving a slightly out-of-focus or three-dimensional effect.

If a textured screen is printed in black over a paler colour, the black will completely obliterate the colour underneath, leaving it showing through the unprinted areas. This can be particularly effective when a shaded or graded area of colour is printed first, and a black textured or patterned screen is printed over the top.

A wax candle is the best medium to use to take rubbings directly onto a screen. As wax is virtually transparent, it does not have any colour to clash with the print-paste.

The method of using rubbings as a resist to permanent coatings is outlined under 'Grease resist', p. 129.

Blottings which are taken to transfer colour, texture, and pattern from a wet surface to a dry one are among the most interesting. They can produce many delicate and unexpected forms – strange eerie landscapes and a variety of fern-like textures (see Fig. 5.46)

Blottings can be taken in this way from any wet printed or painted surface. The surface should be covered in print-paste, and the paper (or cloth) laid lightly on top of it. By very gently stroking the paper the wet print-paste will be transferred to it. If long pools of colour are left in the screen, or accidentally dropped on the cloth, it is always worth while to blot them off with clean spare paper to see what results can be achieved. The results of chance and accident are never to be ignored in any design field!

Textured surfaces also have many pleasant surprises to yield when covered in print-paste. Slightly crinkled surfaces such as masking tape which have been used as a stencil or mask produce an interesting texture when blotted onto an absorbent surface such as newsprint.

Actual objects such as tape and folded ribbon can also be coated in print-paste and rubbed or rollered down onto another surface (see Fig. 5.47). This technique takes us into the realms of transfer printing (see p. 218).

Fig. 5.46 Blotting from wet surfaces.
(a) From pieces of tape on glass which have been coated in print-paste
(b) From a wet paper print

(c) An eerie landscape created from a blotting off a pool of print-paste

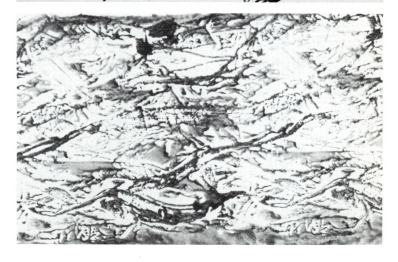

Fig. 5.47 Rag rolling. A ribbon-covered roller is coated in print-paste, and a pattern rollered on to the cloth

Powder resist

Another type of resist that produces unusual and interesting results is powder. Powder prints form mottled or dappled effects that suggest clouds, constellations, or puffs of smoke. The powder can be used to create a random build-up of colour and texture that can also be contained when used in conjunction with other types of more rigid stencil. Any powder that does not congeal in water can be used as a resist. Talcum powder or dusting powder are ideal.

Procedure
1. Sprinkle the powder onto the cloth. It may be necessary to shake it through a sieve to obtain the required effect. Small heaps of powder should not be so high that they raise the screen mesh from the cloth, neither should areas of powder be too fine, or they will not resist the print-paste. (Experiment first!)
2. Place the screen carefully over the powder, taking care not to smudge it. Print the screen.
3. Wash the screen, hosing it well on the inside to blast the powder away from the face side. Do not attempt to hose the face side until all the powder has been washed off.
4. Blot and dry the screen.
5. Leave the print to dry completely. Do not attempt to remove the powder while the print is still damp.
6. When the print is dry it can be carefully ironed in the following way. Without removing the fabric from the table, lay a piece of clean newsprint over it, and iron with a hot iron, displacing as little powder as possible. The powder can then be brushed off or the fabric wiped *gently* with a

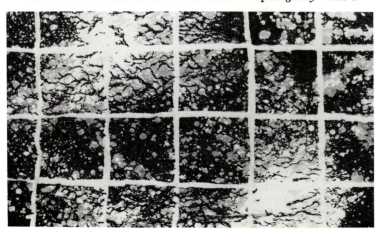

Fig. 5.48 A two-colour powder print used with a screen bearing a grid pattern

Fig. 5.49

Fig. 5.50(a)

Fig. 5.50(b)

Fig. 5.49 Using powder, a small textured area can be created in a larger coloured area

Fig. 5.50 (a) The powder, in this case, has been sprinkled through a circular mask which has been left in position during printing (b) A two-colour powder print produced using both parts of the mask. The powdered printed area is first printed through the hole, and the circle then used to protect the powdered area while the background is printed

damp cloth. Small printed and powdered samples can be lifted and shaken.

Powder prints can be used in several different ways; as detailed below.

1. The whole effect achieved on the first print can be almost exactly repeated due to the fact that the power is held on-to the screen by the print-paste. The screen can then be replaced and reprinted elsewhere.
2. The powder can be sprinkled all over the fabric, but the patterning contained within specific areas by using a screen which has a permanent stencil attached. (see Fig. 5.48).
3. Small areas of texture can be formed within larger areas of colour by scattering the powder through a mask and then removing the mask, and printing a large blank screen over the whole area (see Figs. 5.49). Masks can also be used with powder in other ways.
4. The powder can be used simply to create a textured area on top of a previously printed flat colour: the colour is printed first, left to dry, and then powdered and overprinted with another colour.
5. The most interesting effect, and one that can be used with all the previously mentioned methods is that produced by layering powder and colour to form a texture that exists visually on several levels. This is produced as follows:
   (a) Powder the selected area sparingly, and print the screen, using a pale colour. Wash and dry the screen, and wait for the print to dry.
   (b) Do not remove the remaining powder, but look at the print and decide which areas are least successful, and which areas you would like to preserve. The areas that are to be kept must be repowdered. This second coating of powder will preserve anything that is underneath it.

If you wish to form a texture over a plain printed area, scatter more powder over that area also.

(c) Reprint the screen a second time, using a darker or stronger colour.

(d) Wash and dry the screen, and leave the print to dry.

As most of the powder picks up with the screen it is worth while taking a second print before the screen is washed. This could be done on clean paper, and used to experiment with before taking the next print on cloth. Powder prints can be very successful on paper, as the powder is easy to remove from the paper. As with all techniques, interesting things can be done with the print once it is complete (Fig. 5.51).

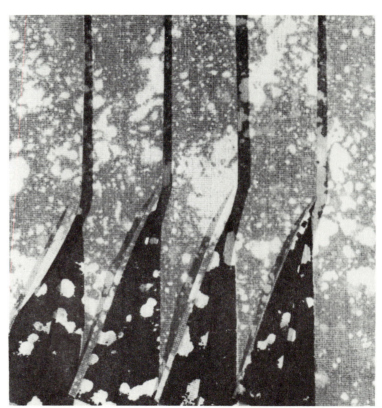

Fig. 5.51 A fabric sample, masked in stripes with powder and tape, and later pleated

Marbling

The method which is used to produce marbled patterns on paper can also be used on small pieces of cloth such as ribbon.

It involves the use of waterproof inks or dyes which are floated on water. The pattern made by the inks on the surface of the water is transferred to the cloth or paper when it is laid on the water.

Spirit-based dyes are not normally used on cloth because: (a) they are not washable; and (b) they leave the cloth feeling stiff and rubbery. Consequently, this type of marbling should not be used over large areas of fabric.

A type of marbling can, however, be produced over a sizeable area of cloth using a screen and normal print-paste. An area can be marbled that is the same size as the screen.

Procedure

1. Choose colours and tones that are not too close in value as these will become indistinct when mixed and the marbled effect will not be visible.
2. Lay pools of colour next to each other in the dye-well (see Fig. 5.52).
3. Using a fine-pointed object carefully mix the pools of colour together to form distinct swirls.
4. Place the screen in position on the cloth and print the screen *once* in the normal way. A strong marbled pattern will occur at the top end of the screen, and will blend towards the bottom.

If the marbled effect is required over a larger area the colour can be placed along the long side of the screen, and pulled sideways across it, using a larger squeegee.

The soft blending into which the marbling eventually disappears is attractive in its own right, and can be produced all over the cloth by printing the unblended pools of colour. This method produces soft stripes that can be straight or curved. Curved lines are formed by using a slightly shorter squeegee than normal, and moving it from side to side as it crosses the screen (see Fig. 5.56).

Marbling and striping can also be used in conjunction with a stencil to form a localised or fragmented pattern (see Fig. 5.53).

Colour grading/shading

The grading of colour or tone in screen printing is a very useful effect. It produces blended tonal ranges, fading intensity, and even three-dimensional effects if carefully controlled.

Tonal ranges can be produced in several ways as follows:

Fig. 5.52 Whirling the pools of colour together in the screen to produce marbling

(a) By photo-mechanical methods used in industry.
(b) By the use of a photographic half-tone. This produces an effect most commonly seen in one-colour (usually black-and-white) newspaper photographs and can be screen printed (see Fig. 5.16).

Fig. 5.53 A marbled pattern printed through a grid-patterned screen.

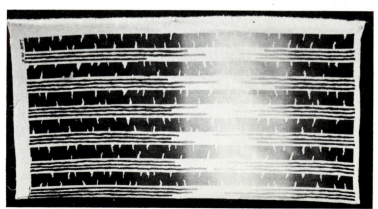

Fig. 5.54 Colour grading. Design by Laurie McIntosh.

(c) By the use of a spray gun (see Fig. 9.19).

(d) By hand stippling on to Kodatrace (see Fig. 5.55).

(e) By tonal transfers used on Kodatrace (see Fig. 5.13).

Tone can also be produced by printing a graduated range of tones simultaneously, in the same way that striping is produced. Very careful colour mixing is necessary if this method is to be successful. If the transition between colours or tones is too great they will form stripes with visible edges.

In any range that progresses from medium to light, medium to dark, or from one colour to another, a group of five or six (if not more) intermediate tones or shades will be

Fig. 5.55 Hand stippling of opaque on Kodatrace can suggest tone. Design by Sarah Wheeler.

needed. The larger the range of tones or shades, the more subtle the effect will be.

The pools of print-paste must always be positioned in sequence in the screen, although the whole sequence can be repeated in the same screen if the screen is large enough, producing a light to dark to light effect, for example.

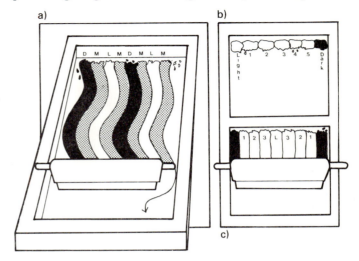

Fig. 5.56 Colour gradation. Positioning tones in the screen in the correct order.
(a) Dark, medium, light, to make dark to light shaded stripes
(b) Dark, medium, light, to make a shaded area
(c) Dark to light to dark

Procedure

1. Lay out at least four large sheets of white paper (newsprint will do). These are used as a surface on which to take strike-offs before the screen is placed on the cloth. The stripes of colour are blended on the paper, and produce a soft shaded effect when the screen is printed on the cloth.

2. Mix a close range of tones or shades. They may range from dark to light, or from one colour to another. Bear in mind that more print-paste than usual is used due to the fact that many strike-offs are taken before the screen is printed on the fabric.

3. Place the screen on one of the large sheets of newsprint. Lay pools of colour, in the correct sequence in the dye-well of the screen (see Fig. 5.56). Squeegee the colour across the screen. It will form stripes. Keeping the stripes of colour on the squeegee blade in line with the stripes that have printed, pull the colour back again across the screen.

4. Lift the screen, and place it on a clean piece of newsprint. Repeat the printing procedure.

5. When the colour has blended to the degree at which no hard stripes are visible, the screen can be placed in position on the cloth and printed.

Each time fresh colour is added, the screen must be printed on newsprint to absorb the stripes that occur from the unblended colour.

These graded tones can look very impressive if combined with geometric, realistic three-dimensional, or architectural type designs. Such designs lend themselves to being quilted and stuffed, and can be pleated or cut and rewoven to good effect.

Wet on wet

Any design can be printed on to a damp fabric, giving soft bleeding edges and outlines. The amount of bleed depends upon the degree to which the cloth has been dampened. The best method for dampening the cloth evenly is to spray water

Fig. 5.57 Wet on wet print.
Design by Martine Vevers

on to it, using a spray gun or a plant spray, once it is fixed to the table. Tests can be carried out with a small screen on parts of the fabric which have been wetted to various degrees.

Dampened fabric can be used in one of two different situations in fabric printing: (a) the fabric can be dampened entirely so that a whole print consists of soft shapes; or (b) it can be selectively dampened so that only certain shapes bleed (e.g. part way through a print). In this case, the parts that are to remain hard-edged must be ironed thoroughly before water is sprayed near or over them.

A CATALOGUE OF DISASTERS!

It is frustrating to make irreversible mistakes, and even more frustrating when you are not sure what caused them!

In printing, many mistakes are reversible; at worst they can be covered up, at best they can be remedied; and at least they can be avoided in future.

Kodatrace

1. **Blobs, smudges and errors.** Remove with water, or methylated spirits if a wax crayon has been used. (Cotton wool buds can be useful here.) Abrasive soap pads can be used for extremely stubborn marks.

2. **Greasy patches causing the opaque to settle unevenly.** Rub the greasy parts of the Kodatrace with a liquid soap or a meths-dampened cloth.

3. **Small tears or cuts.** Cover small rips across the back of the Kodatrace with clear tape. Film with large rips should not be used for repeating designs, as the tear will distort the design.

4. **Deep creases or folds in the Kodatrace.** Do not use deeply creased Kodatrace for repeating designs. Creased drafting film should be avoided wherever possible.

5. **Stained or marked Kodatrace.** A light stain on the Kodatrace from a preceding design will not cause any problems during subsequent exposure with another design. However, if the mark is very opaque, attempts should be made to remove it.

Stenplex Amber

1. **Unwanted slight cuts or over-shooting of edges.** Remedy small cuts at the time of varnishing once the Stenplex Amber has been ironed to the screen. Make sure all cuts are blocked with varnish.
Deep and large cuts will distort the design.

2. **The Stenplex Amber does not adhere to the screen mesh.** This is due to the temperature of the iron, which is too low.

Photographic screen exposure

1. **Blobs and runs in the coating which are visible when dry.** Ignore blobs and runs that are not prominent and do not occur in an area that is to be washed out. Those which do occur in a large area of open mesh can often be hosed out, or blasted out with a needle-jet water gun.
Blobs are the result of:
(a) Too loose a screen mesh.
(b) Too slack a contact between the screen mesh and the coating trough.
(c) Insufficient care when scraping off excess liquid during coating.
(d) Screen coating is too liquid.

2. **The image on the screen does not wash out properly, leaving the mesh blocked**
This is the result of:
(a) Too long an exposure.
(b) Exposure of the screen to light before the Kodatrace was placed on it.
(c) Insufficiently dense painted areas on the Kodatrace.

If it is just a fine film of coating that forms the blockage it can usually be removed by gently hosing it with water, or by careful rubbing with a rag or sponge. It there is a heavy blockage, the screen should be bleached and re-exposed.

The best remedy is, where possible, to blast out the blockage with a needle-jet gun. Should the jet overshoot and break the screen coating the broken area can be repainted in later with the coating.

When blasting along a straight line with a needle jet, it is wise to build up several layers of masking tape against which to blast. This tape will withstand a short attack, although the needle jet is so powerful that it should not be directed at any part that is not intended to be broken down. (it should go without saying that the needle jet should *never* be directed at a person, and that is should be used with great care).

3. The screen does not fit in repeat while being set up on the print table
This is a result of:
(a) Registration guidelines having been drawn inaccurately on the design.
(b) The crosses on the Kodatrace having been misaligned with the grid on the print table during registration.
(c) Insufficient care having been taken when painting shapes along the join-line of the repeat on the Kodatrace.

Remedies
(a) Look at the Kodatrace on the grid. Check that the two crosses are on the same major grid line. Check the pencilled guidelines: these should also both be on the same grid line. If the registration pencil lines are accurate but the crosses are not in line and the repeat still does not fit, check the repeat as outlined under 'Registration of screens', p. 112.
(b) If the design and the repeat are checked and found to be 'square', but the design on the screen still fits oddly, or overlaps the Kodatrace unevenly, this is due to careless painting of the Kodatrace, and can be remedied in the following way. Overlap the screen with the Kodatrace so that it fits to your (relative) satisfaction. Trace the overlap through from the kodatrace on to the screen with a pencil. These overlapping edges can then be either blasted out carefully with a needle-jet gun, or painted out with lactic acid which dissolves the coating. It may also be necessary to paint in other areas with screen coating where unexpected gaps occur.

Fixing the cloth to the print table

1. The fabric does not stick to the table.
(a) The fabric may be incompatible with the table gum that has been used.
(b) The iron may be too cool or too hot.
(c) The gum may have been spread too thickly.

Remedies
(a) Check the fibre content of the fabric.
(b) Spray the cloth with a fine spray of water, and/or adjust temperature of iron.
(c) Scrub down the table to reduce the thickness of the gum.

2. **Creases and scallops that occur during ironing.** Small creases or wrinkles that occur during ironing can be lifted, smoothed, and carefully reironed. If attention is paid to the correct ironing procedure large wrinkles will not occur.

3. **Scallops and deep tension lines that appear during pinning.** This effect is caused by pulling the cloth too tightly. Pull the cloth evenly so that it lies straight between the pins and does not cause strong 'pulls' across its width.

Printing

1. **Patchiness, streaking, uneven colour.** This is caused by careless mixing of the binder and colour, or by an uneven squeegee blade.
    Remix the colour, transferring it to another bowl, and straining it through a piece of screen mesh, and check the squeegee blade.

2. **Strongly coloured blotches and uneven colour.** If old pigments are used, they often form into blobs of concentrated colour that are difficult to disperse.
    Strain the pigment/binder mixture through a piece of screen mesh, and stir thoroughly, using a flexible spatula, or an electric mixer if possible.

3. **Tiny dots of colour appearing on unprinted areas during printing.** These are caused by 'pinholes' in the screen coating, and should have been touched out with screen coating before printing.
    It may also be, if the screen has been printed successfully before, that it has been rubbed over-enthusiastically during washing, causing the coating to break away.

4. **White unprinted areas in the middle of colour.**
This could be caused by:
(a) Varnish that has not been removed from a Stenplex Amber screen.
(b) Insufficient washing and checking of a photographic screen after exposure or printing.
(c) Not enough print-paste being used.

5. **Shadowy double images.** If the screen has moved during printing, or if it has rested on top of a wet printed image, a double image will occur. This cannot be remedied, but in future hold the screen steady while printing (enlist a

helper) and check the previously printed image to ensure that it is dry before putting the screen down again.

6. **Printed lines of colour along the selvage or across the cloth.** This is due to inadequate gumstrip, leaving gaps through which colour can penetrate.

7. **The fabric lifts from the table after printing.** Some swelling of the fabric often takes place during printing, and the fabric usually shrinks back into place. Areas that lift in the middle of a large printed area can be carefully re-pressed. with a warm iron if they do not shrink back naturally.

   If the fabric lifts at the side it can be retaped, reironed, or repinned.

8. **Gaps between colours.** This is caused by an insufficient overlap on the shapes painted on the Kodatraces. White gaps on the cloth, if they are small, can be painted in carefully with the pigment print-paste.

9. **The colours or repeats overlap, or leave an unnaturally large gap.**
This may vary on each repeat and is caused by:
(a) An inconsistent distance between the stops.
(b) The screen bracket being placed on the wrong side of the stop (this causes a 2–3 cm overlap or gap).
(c) The screen bracket may be slightly loose, or the stops (or an individual stop) may be slightly loose.
(d) The registration bar may be uneven where the bolts touch it.

10. **Bleeding: the dye seeps under the screen.**
This is caused by:
(a) The squeegee being held at the wrong angle.
(b) Too loose a screen mesh.
(c) A fabric being printed that is too thin, and requires a back-cloth.
(d) Too runny a print paste.
(e) The squeegee being pulled too many times across the screen.
(f) A pool of dye being left on an area of open mesh (e.g. over the edge of the dye-well).
(g) The over-use of a paper pick-up stencil which has become wet.

11. **The design prints off the fabric at one selvage.** This is a result of not placing the cloth close enough to, or far enough from, the edge of the table, or of setting the design up out of square.

12. **The design has an increasingly wide gap between the repeats.** If the screen screws are not adjusted properly, a gap will occur that is wider at one side of the cloth than the other. An obstruction on the bar will also cause a gap in the print.

13. **Faded or disintegrated edges around a printed shape.** If an object or a paper stencil is being used, blurred edges will occur if the object is too thick, or if more than two sheets of paper are used. A thick object or wad of paper raises the screen mesh from the table and prevents and all-over contact being made between the mesh and the fabric. It could also be caused by too light a squeegee pressure.

14. **Jagged edges on a diagonal printed line.** When a diagonal line is exposed on to a coarse screen mesh the line crosses the mesh in such a way that a 'saw' edge is formed.

Remedy
Use a finer mesh for designs that have strong, hard-edged diagonal features.

15. **The screen mesh tears, due to accident.** A tautly stretched mesh is easily pierced by a sharp object. Small tears in the coated area can be patched with masking tape on the face side. Large tears distort the design, and in this case the mesh should be abandoned. (It can be cut down and used to cover a smaller screen.) If small tears occur in an open area of mesh the design can be printed normally.

16. **Fine lines block on the screen while printing, or print unevenly.** When printing fine lines, speed is of the essence, especially when using pigments. Blocking of fine lines can occur very quickly due to the viscosity and drying rate of the print-paste.

Remedy
(a) Continually print through the screen to avoid blocking, even if this has to be done on newsprint in between prints.
(b) Do not use the screen in a hot room or near a fan heater.

17. **Lines do not print clearly.** A blunt squeegee can often produce less than sharp images. Sharpen the squeegee with fine glasspaper, or use a squeegee dresser.

18. **The surface of the print looks thick and rubbery.** This is due to too high a concentration of pigment colour in the binder.

19. **The colour looks pale and weak, and does not give a dense enough coverage.** This effect comes about when not enough print paste is applied to the cloth on each repeat. The remedy is to pull the squeegee more times across the screen on each strike-off. Alternatively, more pressure may be needed on the squeegee.

20. **The colour flakes or peels off the print after the fabric has been in use for some time.** Rubbing or peeling of colour often occurs when too many layers of colour are built up on an overprint. The maximum amount of layers that should be considered practical when using pigment colours is three.

21. **Unwanted blobs or mistakes on the cloth.** White pigment is useful here to cover small specks or blobs of unwanted colour.

Remedy

Wait until the spots of colour are dry. In the meantime, mix a high percentage of opaque white pigment with the binder. Test it for colour matching on the cloth as whites can vary a great deal. Carefully mix minute quantities of other (already mixed) colours into it until the exact shade of white is reached. Use this to paint over small mistakes. Two layers may be needed to give good coverage.

Used over a large area white pigment will prove rubbery, so it should only be used to cover small mistakes. On silk, or shiny fabrics white pigment can sometimes look more noticeable than the mistake, so be warned!

Sometimes it is possible to incorporate mistakes into a design. Often, where practical to do so, this is the most successful way of covering them.

If they are pale, mistakes can sometimes be covered over with a darker colour. This is best printed (rather than painted) through a shape on a permanent stencil, or with paper pick-ups. It is easy to incorporate a new shape into a design if it can be made to bear some relation to other shapes already in existence. It may even be necessary to repeat the area that covers the mistake if it occurs on a repeating design!

The use of black pigment is the best method for covering mistakes, and in designs that incorporate a lot of black, one or more additional black shapes can sometimes be added without appearing too noticeable.

Mistakes can lead to exciting new effects and techniques, and so can have a positive, as well as a negative side.

CHAPTER 6

Dyeing

DYEING: BASIC EQUIPMENT

Dyeing can be carried out with the most basic equipment. The tools needed are listed below, and can be modified to suit individual requirements.

Fig. 6.1 Dyeing equipment

149

A set of metric scales should be bought by the serious dyer, as measurement by volume (i.e. spoonfuls, etc.) is inaccurate when dealing with small amounts of dye and fine colour matching.

Litre flasks and glass beakers of various sizes, stainless steel spoons, and wooden rods will be required. Wooden rods should be carefully sanded to a rounded end to avoid damaging delicate fabrics.

A collection of bowls and containers of different types will be useful, as often when carrying out experiments, several bowls are needed at one time. Glass bowls are rather delicate, and should not be used unless they are heat-proof. Enamel vessels should also be avoided, as they chip easily. When enamel vessels become chipped they absorb dye which then is released in the next dye bath. Stainless steel should be used wherever possible.

A container large enough to hold at least 9 litres of water per 0.5 kg of fabric is a must. (Secondhand shops can be a boon here, selling large boilers, preserving saucepans, and old industrial tea-urns.) If hot dyes are to be used the container must be made of metal. If cold dyes are to be used, any large plastic container will be suitable. A stock of abrasive detergent and wire wool should be kept to hand, as all pans used for dyeing must be scrubbed vigorously to remove traces of dye.

A dyeing thermometer or a sugar-boiling thermometer will be needed if using dyes which must be carefully temperature controlled. Such thermometers can be obtained from specialist suppliers, or, more easily, from hardware shops.

Most dyes, while not completely fixed before the dyeing process is complete, show an alarming capacity for permanence when splashed on to clothing. A wise investment is an all-enveloping boiler suit or overall! Large sheets of polythene are also useful, to avoid dye splashes if working in the home. Rubber gloves should also be used, and fine surgical gloves, which are more practical than the domestic variety, can be obtained from chemist shops and drug-stores.

Home-dyers might wish to follow some manufacturers' directions, and use a washing machine for dyeing. With dyes that are specified for use in a washing machine this is a possibility. A small boiler is an alternative if a quantity of dyeing is to be carried out. A 36-litre capacity domestic boiler can be used to dye 3 m of 90 cm wide medium-weight cotton, or 5 m of lightweight silk with ease. (A boiler can also be used in some steaming processes to fix dye or print-paste.)

Bunsen burners are generally used in dye labs for the purpose of heating small amounts of water. However, a small single or double electric hotplate is equally practical, and more stable, which is important where the heating of wax is concerned.

DYES AND DYEING

A wide range of dyes is available today, making it possible for the non-professional craftsman to colour a variety of fabrics. This, coupled with the fact that many commercial dyes can be obtained from some suppliers in small quantities makes the whole business of domestic dyeing much more exciting.

However, the prospect of using commercial dyes can seem daunting to the beginner due to the fact that the choice of dyes is so vast. The same type, or 'class' of dye may be produced by different manufacturers, each of whom give it a personal trade name. Additives used with the dyes are also often individually named in this way, making dye recipes seem more complicated than they actually are. Once the individual trade names, and even the actual names of some chemicals are deciphered, they can often be found to be substances that are in common use in the home, or basic compounds that are readily available from chemists or hardware stores, sold under familiar names. Suddenly, dye recipes seem less formidable!

The quickest and most easily achieved results will be produced using domestic dyes, which are easily obtained in small quantities and a wide range of colours. They are easy to use, and require only the addition of salt or soda to fix them.

Dylon dyes are the domestic dyes most commonly available in the UK. Dylon hot dyes can be applied with varying degrees of success to most fibres, including nylon, cotton, wool and linen, silk, velvet and polyester, Tricel, Lycra, and viscose rayon.

Ranges of domestic dyes such as Dylon often include a selection of cold dyes and additives that make them suitable for use on a variety of fabrics, and in many different techniques.

Dylon cold dye is suitable for batik and other resist work, and can be adapted for hand painting by the addition of 'Paintex' and dye fix. When thickened, Dylon cold dyes can even be used for screen and block printing. (Similar types of domestic dyes and additives may be marketed under different names in different countries.) However, if any quantity of dyeing is to be carried out, it is, in the long run, more economical to invest in a range of commercial dyes. Although commercial dyes are not marketed in such a large range of shades as domestic dyes, colour mixtures are easy to achieve, and, because such dyes are highly concentrated, less dye is needed to produce stronger colour. In some instances, dyes from different manufacturers can be mixed together, provided that they are of the same class of dye (check with suppliers).

Dyes are divided into 'classes' according to their affinity

with particular fabrics. It is important to ascertain the exact composition of a fabric before attempting to dye it, as a dye will not produce good results if used on an unsuitable fabric.

Main classes of dye: some trade names and manufacturers

Acid dyes; suitable for wool and silk.

Trade names:	Lissamine	Coomassie	Supranol
Manufacturers:	ICI	ICI	Bayer

Direct dyes; suitable for cellulosic fibres, i.e. cotton, linen, viscose rayon.

Trade names:	Chlorozol	Durazol	Suprexel	Paramine
Manufacturers:	ICI	ICI	L.B. Holliday	L.B. Holliday

(Selected direct dyes are also suitable for silk, wool, and nylon)

Reactive dyes; also suitable for cellulosic fibres.

Trade names:	Procion	Cibacron
Manufacturers:	ICI	Ciba/Geigy

Disperse dyes; suitable for polyester, acrylic, nylon.

Trade names:	Supracet	Polycron	Dispersol
Manufacturers:	L.B. Holliday	L.B. Holliday	ICI

The choice of dye will obviously depend upon the type of work that is to be carried out, and the kind of dyeing methods that are to be used.

The craftsperson generally uses dyes in one of several ways:

(a) For immersion dyeing, in which the whole cloth is evenly coloured.
(b) For dip-dyeing, in which parts of the cloth are coloured.
(c) For hand painting.
(d) With a resist such as wax.

The dyes used for one of these methods may not be suitable for another.

The comparative costs of the various dyes will also influence the choice, as will their shelf life and any complexities involved in their use. Each type of dye has its own advantages, and its own drawbacks.

Assuming that most people choose to work on natural fibres, the choice of dyes is limited to those that are suitable for silk, wool, cotton, linen, and viscose rayon. Thus, in this case the dyes most suitable are direct dyes, reactive dyes, and acid dyes.

Direct dyes are relatively cheap to buy, and easy and successful when used for normal immersion dyeing. However, they must be used hot, and are not, therefore, suitable for use with a wax resist. Also, they cannot be used as a concentrate, and this makes them unsuitable for dip-dyeing or hand painting.

Acid dyes will give the most brilliant colours on silk and can be mixed to a concentrate and used cold. They do, however, require fixing by steaming.

Reactive dyes give strong, fast colour on cellulosic fibres. They must not be used hot, but can be mixed to a concentrate. This makes them eminently suitable for use with a resist, and in dip-dyeing methods. Reactive dyes also require fixing, but this is a relatively easy matter.

So, if you can plan what type the majority of your work is to be, you can make your choice as to which dye to use.

Preparation of the fabric prior to dyeing

In all cases of dyeing or printing the quality of the end-product is proportionate to the care taken with the choice of, or pretreatment of, the fabric prior to printing or dyeing.

If possible, only scoured and bleached fabrics *specifically marked* as being prepared for printing and dyeing should be used. These can be obtained from specialist suppliers (see UK suppliers, p. 240).

Remember that snow-white fabrics usually contain optical bleaches which are added with a resin finish. Obviously, these additives will affect any dyes used with them.

If fabrics are bought retail, small samples should be obtained first, and tested to determine their composition and how they dye. Particular care should be taken when choosing cotton, as many a 'cotton' has turned out to be a cotton/polyester mix that has dyed unevenly.

If fabric is not specifically prepared for printing and dyeing it must be scoured. Scouring is simply the energetic washing of the fabric in a recommended solution.

Scouring procedure
1. Dissolve 1–2 parts Lissapol D powder to every 1,000 parts of water heated to 70–80 °C (158–176 °F). A sugar-boiling thermometer will be useful during this, and all following procedures.

2. Work the fabric around in this mixture for about 30 minutes.
3. Rinse thoroughly in warm, and then cold running water.

OR

If Lissapol D powder is not available, scour the fabric at, or near the boil in a solution consisting of 1 cup of washing soda, or $\frac{1}{2}$ cup of sodium carbonate per 4.5 litres of water, for 30–60 minutes.

If a washing machine can be used, a small amount (just a squirt) of washing-up liquid can be added to the water and soda, and this will help the scouring.

DYEING: LIQUOR RATIOS, AND DYE PERCENTAGES

When dyeing, it is necessary to use a particular ratio of water to cloth. The ratio of water to cloth must be calculated carefully, as it is important for several reasons:

(a) If too little water is used, blotchy dyeing will result.
(b) If too much water is used, the dyeing time will be unnecessarily prolonged.
(c) If a fixing agent is being used in the dye-bath the amount used often depends upon the volume of water.

It is therefore important to keep a record each time of the amount of water used.

Manufacturers usually recommend a ratio of water to cloth. This can be adjusted as required. These ratios are sometimes described as 'short dye-baths' and 'long dye-baths'. Short dye-baths have a small amount of water to cloth, giving a high concentration of dye and are used for small, quick samples. Long dye-baths have a high ratio of water to cloth and a longer dyeing time and are used for lengths of cloth where even coloration is vital. For the quick dyeing of samples, a ratio of 5 : 1 has been found to be most successful, and for dyeing lengths of cloth, a ratio of 20 : 1 to 40 : 1, i.e. 100 g (grams) of cloth to approximately 3 litres of water. For dyeing yarn a ratio of 15 : 20 : 1 would be used.

As well as the ratio of liquid to cloth, the type and shape of vessel used as a dye-bath is also important. A tall cylindrical vessel may hold as much water as a broad shallow one, but neither may allow enough space for the fabric to be moved around freely.

The amount of dyestuff used must also be calculated carefully, based upon the weight of the dry cloth. Tins of domestic dye contain directions regarding the weight of cloth that can be dyed with each tin of dye. These instructions should be carefully followed. Shade tables can sometimes be obtained from commercial dye manufacturers and suppliers, and are invaluable, as they show strong, medium, and pale shades of each colour. Each shade is produced by using a particular percentage of dye in relation to the weight of cloth. For example, a high percentage of red produces a strong red; a low percentage produces a pink.

It is easy to calculate the amount of dye needed by using multiples of 100 g of cloth: x grams of dye per 100 g of cloth.

The shade table below is issued by ICI, and serves as a rough guide to the use of all dyes. However, it is very important not to apply the 'rules' used with one type of dye to another, possibly different, type. Shade cards and relevant instructions should be obtained from individual manufacturers or suppliers wherever possible, as some dyes reach full strength at a higher or lower percentage than those listed below. (Notably blacks and deep blues: some blacks are used up to 6 per cent, so do check shade cards.)

General percentage shade table
0.5% of dye to cloth: pale shade
1.0% of dye to cloth: medium shade
2.0% of dye to cloth: dark shade

Sample recipe to achieve a medium shade (calculated at 1%)
Weight of cloth	=	500 g
1% dye for medium shade	=	5 g
Water (25 : 1 ratio)	=	12,500 ml (12.5 litres)

Soft water should be used for dyeing (preferably rain-water.) Water softeners such as sodium hexametaphosphate (or Calgon, a domestic water softener) should be used to soften the water, in the proportion of 1 g to every litre of water.★

★ The precise amount of Calgon used depends upon the hardness of the water in a particular area. The following guide might prove useful: when the Calgon has successfully softened the water it should be clear; if the water is still cloudy more Calgon can be added slowly until it clears.

USING DIRECT, REACTIVE, AND ACID DYES

Direct dyes

Most dyes involve the use of a 'carrier' to make them take on the fabric. The carrier used with direct dyes is common salt. The amount of salt used is based, like the dyestuff, on the weight of the dry cloth, but is also determined by whether a light, medium, or dark shade is to be dyed.

If a *light shade* is to be dyed calculate the amount of salt at 5 per cent of the dry weight of the cloth.

If a *medium shade* is to be dyed the salt should be calculated at 10 per cent of the dry weight of the cloth.

If a *dark shade* is to be dyed the salt should be 20 per cent of the dry weight of the cloth.

You will need:

Dyestuff:	$x\%$	calculated on the dry weight of cloth
Salt:	$x\%$	calculated on the dry weight of cloth and depth of shade required
Water:	25 : 1 to 40 : 1 liquor ratio	calculated on the dry weight of cloth

Procedure

1. Heat the water in the dye-bath.
2. Paste the dyestuff with a little soft water, and dissolve with about 150 ml of boiling water until all lumps are dispersed. Boil it, and strain if neccessary.
3. When the temperature in the dyebath reaches 37 °C (100 °F) add one-third of the salt.
4. When the water reaches 48 °C (120 °F) add all the dye; stir well.
5. Quickly immerse the wetted fabric, opening it out as much as possible and agitate it in the dye-bath. Bring it to the boil and stir for about 10 minutes.
6. Remove the fabric, and stir in another one-third of the salt.
7. Replace the fabric and stir for another 10–15 minutes.
8. Remove the fabric again, add the last of the salt, replace the fabric, and continue boiling.
9. When the required colour is reached, remove and rinse the fabric until the water runs clear.

Fixing agents can be obtained from suppliers for use with direct dyes, if required. They are applied after dyeing, and improve the wash fastness of the dyes.

As mentioned previously, direct dyes cannot be used as a concentrate.

Reactive dyes

The most commonly used reactive dye is Procion, manufactured by ICI. The Procoin M range is recommended for use in schools because the dyes are relatively straightforward to use and can be easily fixed. They give good strong colours, and can be mixed to a concentrate for use in situations where immersion dyeing is not suitable (e.g. hand painting and dip-dyeing). Reactive dyes (Procions) are so called because of the chemical reaction that takes place between the fibre and the dye. This reaction is brought about by the addition of an alkali to the dye-bath, and is consolidated during fixing. The alkali used is sodium carbonate (washing soda – sal soda in the USA). The dye will not 'take' on the cloth until the soda has been added. Manufacturers specify that the dye/alkali mixture remains usable for only 2–3 hours. In practice, however, the mixture can last for much longer than this.

Personal experimentation and experience are useful when using reactive dyes. If unwilling to take a chance, follow the manufacturer's instruction to the letter, perhaps keeping dye and alkali mixtures apart until needed, and keeping all dye mixtures in airtight containers. Checks should always be made when using outdated dye liquors, as it is not possible to judge an exhausted dye liquor by eye.

Dyeing with Procion MX dyes

You will need:

Dyestuff:	$x\%$	calculated on the dry weight of cloth
Salt:	30–60	(parts per 1,000 of dye-bath liquor)
Sodium carbonate:	8	(parts per 1,000 of dye-bath liquor)
OR		
Washing soda (sal soda)	20	(parts per 1,000 of dye-bath
Water:	25 : 1	liquor) liquor ratio

1. Paste the dyestuff carefully with a small amount of cool soft water, dispersing any lumps (strain it through gauze if necessary).
2. Heat the water in the dye-bath to 20 °C (68 °F). It must not exceed 30 °C (86 °F).
3. Add the dye to the dye-bath, stirring it well.
4. Add the wetted fabric to the dye-bath, open it out and keep it moving. Stir for 5–10 minutes.
5. Remove the fabric, and stir in one-quarter of the salt. Replace the fabric and stir it for 5–10 minutes.
6. Repeat item 5.
7. Remove the fabric, add the remaining salt, and replace the

fabric. Stir for another 5–10 minutes. The temperature of the water must stay below 40 °C (104 °F).

8. Remove the fabric. Stir in the soda. Replace the fabric, and turn it well for 1 hour. Do not leave the dye-bath during this time, as the fabric must be kept moving.

9. Remove the fabric and rinse it well in warm, and then cold water. A residue of dye will wash out. This is to be expected. Rinse the fabric until the water runs clear.

10. Immerse the fabric in a solution of Lissapol D or detergent in water – 1 g per litre, heated to 80–90 °C (194 °F) – for 15 minutes. If the water becomes highly coloured, discard it and commence the procedure again.

11. Finally, hang the fabric to dry, pulling out any deep creases. Natural fixation of the dye can be brought about by simply hanging the fabric in a warm atmosphere.

Dyeing with acid dyes

You will need:

Dyestuff:	x%	calculated on the dry weight of the cloth
Acetic Acid:	2%	for light to medium shades, calculated on dry weight of cloth
	OR 4%	for dark shades
Water:	40 : 1 to 25 : 1	liquor ratio

1. Heat the water in the dye-bath to 50 °C (120 °F).
2. Paste the dyestuff in a small amount of cool soft water, and add about 150 ml of boiling water to dissolve it (strain it through gauze if necessary).
3. Add half the dye to the dye-bath. Stir. Add wetted fabric.
4. Stir the fabric for 5–10 minutes.
5. Remove the fabric, and add the other half of the dye. Replace the fabric, and stir for a further 5–10 minutes.
6. Remove the fabric, and add half the acid. Replace the fabric and stir for 5 minutes.
7. Remove the fabric again, and add the second half of the acid. Replace the fabric and bring the liquid to the boil. The fabric should boil for between 10 and 30 minutes. At the end of this time the dye-bath should be 'exhausted' and the water should be virtually clear.

Note: With dyeing, as it is always a lengthy procedure, it is tempting to leave the fabric to soak in the dye. It is important, however, *not* to leave the dye-bath. The fabric must be continuously moved around in the dye or blotchy dyeing will result where parts of the fabric sit above the dye on air bubbles, and other parts are tightly compressed in the liquid.

CONCENTRATES

There are situations where it is not practical to immerse fabric in dye for lengths of time: hand painting or dip-dyeing, for example. When using these techniques the dye must be sufficiently concentrated to make an immediate impact on the fabric. Considering that it can take over an hour to immerse dye a piece of fabric, it is not difficult to guess at the concentration of dye needed to colour the cloth on contact! The dye does not have time to penetrate the cloth and produce a strong build-up of colour, and therefore a concentration of dye is needed that will produce the maximum depth of colour in the minimum time.

With most dyes it is not practical to mix them to a concentrate, but fortunately Procion dyes (reactives) and acids can be used in this way, although they will subsequently need to be fixed. As both can also be used cold this is also an advantage as they can be painted over resists that would be melted by hot dyes.

Using acids and reactives means that hand painting can be done on wool, silk, cotton, linen, and viscose rayon.

Acid concentrate

Concentrates are not calculated upon the weight of cloth, but on the amount of liquid required to do the work in hand.

You will need:

Soft water:	50	parts (millilitres)
Water	950	parts (millilitres)
Dyestuff, not to exceed	30	parts (grams)
Ammonium sulphate		
OR		
Ammonium oxalate	15	parts
	1,045	

Mixing the concentrate

1. Paste the dyestuff with the soft water.
2. Add the rest of the water at boiling-point.
3. Add the ammonium oxalate or ammonium sulphate. If a wax resist is being used, wait for the mixture to cool.

Procion concentrate

You will need:

Urea:	25	parts (grams)
Boiling water	300	parts (millilitres)
Dyestuff:	10–50	parts (grams)
Cold water:	540	parts (millilitres)
	900	

Procedure

1. Dissolve the urea in the boiling water, and allow it to cool to 50 °C (122 °F).
2. Paste the Procion dyestuff with this water.
3. Add the remaining cold water.
4. Strain through gauze if necessary.

The dye will not become 'fast' on the fabric until an alkali has been added (sodium carbonate and sodium bicarbonate). Once the alkali has been added the manufacturers specify that the dye will only keep for about 3 hours. (*Note*: Experiment may prove otherwise.)

The alkali is mixed as follows:

Sodium carbonate	4 parts
Washing soda (sal soda)	8 parts

Warm water to bulk to 100 parts is used to dissolve the soda. The alkali can be mixed and kept separate from the dye mix. It can then be added in proportionate amounts as work progresses, and the dye solution will keep longer.

Alternatively, the alkali can be kept permanently separate from the dye mix and *brushed* over painted parts of the fabric when the dye is dry. If a build-up of colour is being formed by painting layers on top of each other the fabric should be rinsed after each layer of alkali has dried over the previously painted colour.

Fixing

Both acid and reactive concentrates require fixing.

Fixing fabrics painted with Procion concentrate

Fixing Procion concentrate is a relatively simple matter, the method chosen depending upon whether or not a resist has been used, as some resists do not stand the application of heat. The most commonly used methods of fixing Procion concentrate are listed under the headings below.

Air hanging. If the fabric is hung in a warm (preferably humid) atmosphere, fixation will take place in about 12 hours. As a precaution, the fabric can also be ironed.

Ironing. The fabric should be ironed slowly, with an iron set to 'hot'. This method is obviously useful in batik, as the wax can be removed from the fabric, and the dye fixed at the same time. The dye should be allowed to dry for several hours (preferably overnight) before the fabric is ironed.

Steaming. If a purpose-built steamer is not available, the fabric can be steamed over a boiler or in a drying cabinet into which steam is blown from an electric kettle. The fabric should be wrapped loosely, and hung above the source of the steam.

Baking. Many colleges have baking cabinets which are used to fix pigments. Whereas pigments must never be baked in a domestic oven, Procion dyes can be fixed in this way if a baker is not available.

The fabric should be wrapped in a cloth very loosely, and placed in an electric oven set to 140 °C (285 °F) and baked for 5 minutes.

Tumble dryers. The intrepid dyer who is not averse to dye particles appearing in the tumble dryer can fix fabrics in this way. The dryer must be set to 'hot', and the fabric tumbled in it for 20 minutes.

In most cases, air-hanging and ironing will prove to be the most convenient ways of fixing the dye, especially if a wax resist has been used.

Fixing fabrics coloured with acid concentrate

Fabrics coloured with acid concentrates (or printed with acid dyes) require steaming to fix them.

Special steaming units are used in industry, and these steam fabrics under pressure. Smaller versions are often used in art schools. Very small fabric samples can be steam-fixed as shown in Fig. 6.2. The steaming of larger pieces of fabric is

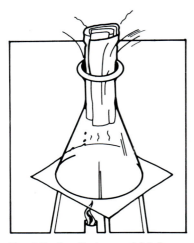

Fig. 6.2 Small pieces of fabric can be wrapped in a piece of thick cloth and steamed in the neck of a laboratory flask to fix them

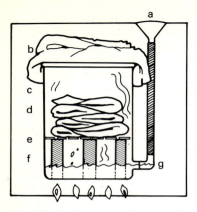

Fig. 6.3 An improvised 'steamer' made from an old tea-urn.
(a) A funnel resting in a pipe. The liquid level can be topped up here
(b) A thick blanket on top of the pan-lid. This prevents escape of steam
(c) The urn
(d) The fabric inside, wrapped in a thick piece of blanket
(e) A perforated 'shelf' that allows steam to pass through
(f) Supports that hold the shelf, standing in the water
(g) A transparent insert in the pipe means that the water-level inside the pan can be checked without opening the lid

more problematical, but they *can* be successfully steamed without any specialist equipment, even in the home. A large vessel with a tightly fitting lid will be needed. An old tea-urn with a tap or outlet on it would be ideal, otherwise an ordinary saucepan, a preserving pan, or a domestic boiler could be used (see Fig. 6.3). Do not, under any circumstances use a pressure cooker! If a tea-urn is used, a plastic pipe with a glass insert could be attached to the tap, enabling a check to be kept on the water level, topping it up if necessary.

Whichever vessel is used it should contain enough water to boil for an hour without evaporating. The vessel should also be deep enough for the fabric to be supported above the water level so that it does not come into contact with the boiling water.

The inside of the pan should be arranged as seen in Fig. 6.3, and the fabric steamed for 1 hour. The lid should not be removed from the pan during this time, so experiments should be carried out before the fabric is steamed to determine how much water is needed, and at what height the fabric should be held above the water. If the water touches or splashes the fabric unsightly water marks will occur.

USING DYES

Dyes are like paints, in that they can be mixed together at source to create intermediate shades. However, dyes are normally used like water-colours as, being transparent, they form washes of colour that are clear enough to allow other colours to show through. With water-colours, intense transparent shades can be produced, and painters have often turned to dyes to obtain the powerful luminosity and fluidity of water-colours, coupled with the permanence normally associated with oil paints. Strong dyes are an ideal medium with which to stain canvas!

The transparency of dyes can best be understood by producing a range of dyed samples. A wide colour range of samples can be produced as given below, using either domestic or commercial dyes.

Dyed samples

1. Make up one bowl each of the basic primary colours, plus black, to a concentrate powerful enough to dip-dye.

(Dip-dyeing with a concentrate will save time.)

2. Take one handkerchief-sized sample of cloth (preferably cotton – an old piece of sheeting would be suitable) for each colour, and dip-dye each one a different colour.

3. Blot, dry, and fix the samples, and cut each one into about four strips. (Extra strips can be kept on one side in case they are needed.)

4. Take the strips, and place each one of them in another colour. Leave the end of the cloth out of the dye – hang it over the edge of the bowl, for instance. This will preserve part of the first colour.

5. Again, dry and fix the samples. They can then be dipped into yet another colour in the same way. If each time they are dipped part of the preceding colour is left exposed, it will be easy to see the sequence of dyeing that produces the best results.

You will find that although you may keep all the samples in the dye for the same length of time, different results will occur. It may be necessary to use the same pair of colours in different sequences to discover which should be applied first to achieve the best results. Some dyes will take much faster and more strongly than others, and this is very important when mixing secondary and tertiary shades by over-dyeing. For example, to form an orange, the best results might be achieved if a cloth dyed yellow is over-dyed with a red, rather than vice versa. To dye a green it may be necessary to dye the cloth blue first, and then over-dye it yellow. Experiment will reveal all!

The dyeing of samples can be taken as far as the size of the samples will allow. Samples can be kept and catalogued, or cut up to form personal shade cards (Figs 6.4 and 6.5). A file of dyed samples should be kept, along with recipes and lists of procedures to which new samples and dye scraps of cloth and yarn can be added.

Many surprises will occur during dyeing, and it will save valuable time and energy if effects are noted for future reference.

One point worth remembering is that the colours look more intense when the fabric is wet than when it is dry. It will save disappointment if the following is noted:

(a) *Cotton*: The colour will be one-third paler when dry.
(b) *Silk*: The colour will be half as strong when dry.
(c) *Wool*: The colour will be almost the same strength dry as wet.
(d) Be especially careful with 'blacks' as they can often dry to a grey!

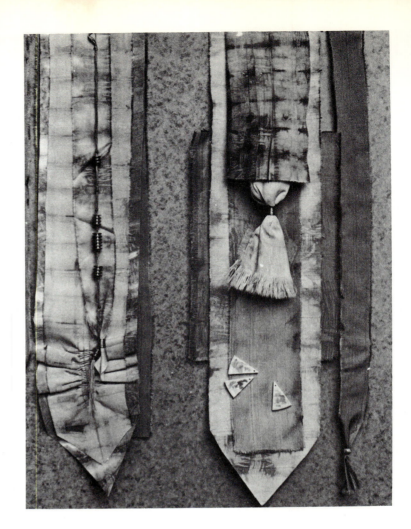

Fig. 6.4 Small left-over dyed
scraps can be made use of

Thickeners

One of the characteristics of using dyes for hand painting is
that they bleed on the cloth. Pigments can be used instead of
dyes to form a harder outline and more controlled shapes.
However, the density of pigments might not always be
desirable. What may be needed is the transparency of dyes,
with the firmness of pigments. Dyes can be thickened to give
this effect, and are used in this form for printing and hand
painting, different consistencies being used for each. (For
recipes see Ch. 9, p. 223.)

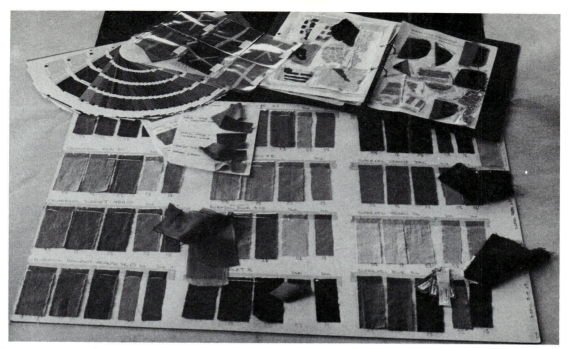

Fig. 6.5   Shade cards

DISCHARGE DYEING

'Discharge' is a term given to a method of decoloration in which colour is removed from selected areas of a previously dyed fabric. The simplest way of discharge dyeing is by the use of bleach.

However, when we talk about 'discharge' we generally refer to the more complex procedures which are used to produce a specific and calculated effect, usually in printing. The subject of discharge printing and dyeing is a very technical one, and specialist textbooks and recipes should be consulted if discharge methods are to be investigated in any depth.

The actual term 'discharge' used in this case, describes a method whereby colour is removed in selected areas from a fabric that has been previously dyed with a dischargeable dye. In printing, the colour is removed by a discharging agent which is printed in the normal way. When the fabric is steamed the discharged pattern becomes apparent. Often the discharging agent carries a colour; one colour is removed and another takes its place. This is the only means by which a dark background can be overprinted with a lighter colour, apart from the use of dense white pigment. This simplistic description masks the fact that discharge printing is a complex procedure, and a great deal of skill (not to mention experience) is needed to produce successful results.

With dyeing the picture is a slightly less complicated one. If recipes are not closely followed the results can be somewhat hit and miss, but it is this very characteristic that can make discharge dyeing so exciting.

Various dye-discharging compounds can be used. Bleach is the most obvious, though not the most predictable, and commercial compounds are the most successful, though not the most easily obtainable.

Bleach as a discharge

Bleach must always be used carefully as it is potentially dangerous. It should be used in a well-ventilated room, and only when wearing rubber gloves. As full-strength bleach can rot fabric very quickly, it is not difficult to see what it can do to the skin. It can also irritate the eyes. However, if used with care, there should be no cause for alarm.

Strong bleach can be painted onto a previously dyed fabric, and spontaneous and successful designs can be produced by this method, especially if two dyeings have taken place, one on top of the other.

If the first dye resists the bleach longer than the second dye, interesting colour combinations and 'haloing' can result

Fig. 6.6 Simple bleach resist on gauze, by Julie Speechley.

where one dye is bleached out more quickly than the other.

The colour can also be taken out by immersing the cloth in a bleach bath. This is usually carried out in conjunction with a resist such as string, as used in tie-dye work (see Fig. 7.16).

It is not possible to suggest an exact ratio of bleach to water, as the strength of different bleaches varies. Experiments could be carried out starting with a ratio of 5 : 1 (5 parts water to 1 part bleach). Too strong a solution will rot the cloth, and too weak a solution will not discharge the colour, so experiment is vital.

Domestic dye-discharging agents

Discharging agents such as Dygon are sold through general retailers. They work well if used according to the manufacturer's instructions, and in conjunction with the right type of dye.

Most commercially dyed fabrics are not dischargeable. Some may be discharged to a greater or lesser degree. As always, experiments with small samples should be carried out before using commercially dyed fabrics.

Commercial stripping agents

Commercial discharging compounds should be used with close attention to the supplier's instructions. This is because in each class of dye (i.e. the *type* of dye that has an affinity with a particular fabric) there are individual dyes which may not be suitable for discharge purposes. There are others that may give excellent results, and some that can only be discharged when used originally at a certain percentage. If close attention is paid to the supplier's recipes, good results can be achieved. It is important to obtain shade cards if possible, and more important, lists of colours suitable for discharge. Most dye manufacturers list the dischargeability of their dyes; they are usually numbered 1–5, or lettered A–E:

A or 5	The dyed fabric discharges to white
B or 4	The dyed fabric is suitable for coloured discharge (i.e. where one colour is replaced by another)
C/D or 3/2	Are not suitable at all
E or 1	Can be used as a discharging colour, i.e. it can be used to take the place of a colour over which it is printed

The discharging agent used is sodium sulphloxylate formaldehyde, sold under the trade names Rongalite and Redusol (among others.) The following recipe makes up a reducing solution suitable for *painting* on:

Reducing agent	200 g
Hot water	100 ml
Glycerine	50 ml
Thickening agent	650 ml

The discharge of the colour does not take place until the fabric has been steamed. The amount of time that the fabric should be steamed depends upon the type of steamer being used, therefore experiments should be carried out to determine the correct steaming time.

A *soaking* solution gives results that can be checked, as the colour discharges in the reducing bath. This method is obviously interesting when used with a string resist, as it produces a negative of the usual results (see Fig. 7.17). It is not, however, suitable for wax resist methods as the liquid in the reducing bath must be used at the boil.

For the reducing bath you will need:

Reducing agent	50 g
Water	2 litres

Heat the mixture to the boil. Place the fabric in it, and continue to boil. Discharge takes place at the boil, so the temperature should not be lowered. The fabric can be removed any time the required reduction of colour is attained.

CHAPTER 7

Tie-dye

Tie-dye is an ancient craft which today still forms a large part of the home textile market in countries such as India and Africa. It is also extremely popular with amateur craftsman everywhere, due to the ease with which distinctive results can be obtained.

It is this very characteristic that has led tie-dye to become something of a cliché in the modern crafts scene. Yet, as with many techniques which are basically uncomplicated, it is possible, once certain preconceptions have been abandoned, to produce designs of great impact and staggering intricacy (see Fig. 7.1).

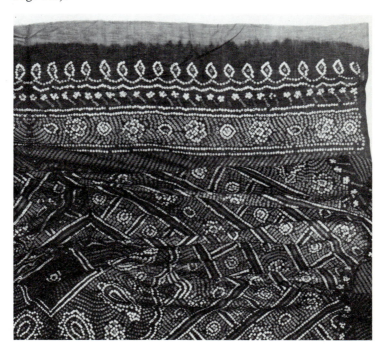

Fig. 7.1 Modern tie-dyed fabric from northern India. The pattern is produced by pressing the fabric on to an arranged bed of nails prior to tying it

Fig. 7.2 The large radiating circle
that typifies tie-dye

The large radiating circle of colour that seems to typify tie-dye in our minds is formed by drawing the fabric up into peaks, and tying and dyeing it (see Fig. 7.2). In the fabric shown in Fig. 7.1 the myriad of tiny dots that form the pattern are produced in the same way, and it is when the large familiar shapes are changed in some way, i.e. reduced, multiplied, or overlaid with other patterns, that the results become more unexpected.

To produce such small intricate patterns the fabric is often folded and pressed on to a bed of nails or pins which have been arranged in a particular formation. The pinholes on the cloth act as guidelines – tiny areas of fabric being drawn up around each one, and tied. In some cases grains of rice or tiny seeds are tied into the cloth. A time-consuming business!

The intricate Japanese and Indian tie-dyed fabrics with their small clearly defined patterns contrast strongly with the direct and powerful effects favoured by the African countries. Tie-dye is found all over Africa, especially in Nigeria, where the best examples are produced by the Yoruba people (see Fig. 7.3). The large shapes which are typical of the African tie-dyes are produced by binding the cloth with a heavy cord, such as raffia.

Fig. 7.3 African tie-dyed fabric

More linear effects and clearer than those made with tie-dye can be produced using a technique known as tri-tik, in which the cloth is *stitched* and dyed (see Fig. 7.4). Tri-tik produces fine puckered lines and small shapes that can be formed into figurative images, unlike the shapes formed with tie-dye which are purely abstract.

DYES

The dye traditionally associated with tie-dye is indigo, which is a vegetable dye, and many rich and subtle colours can also be produced with other vegetable dyes. In most parts of the world, however, considerations of speed, cost and convenience have meant that synthetic dyes have superseded vegetable dyes, thus speeding up traditional techniques and making them more attractive to us, who have little time to spare.

Fig. 7.4 Tri-tik.
(a) Machined tri-tik. The fabric
has been pleated and tightly
zigzagged along the edges of the
pleats

(b) Hand-sewn tri-tik. The fine
stitches can be used to form
figurative images, as well as
abstract ones. Samples by Julie
Speechley

Each textile technique has certain characteristics that dictate the type of dyes that must be used. What is normally required when working with a direct resist (in this case, the cord) is the maximum coloration in the minimum time. This is sometimes achieved by painting the cloth with a concentrated dye, as if it is not actually immersed in a dye there is less chance that the dye will penetrate the resist.

With tie-dye the picture is a different one. Unless the cloth *is* immersed in a dye-bath the dye will not soak through the many layers of folded fabric. This problem is solved by quickly dip-dyeing the tied fabric in the same concentrate as used for painting. Thus the fabric can be saturation dyed very quickly.

Reactive dyes are most suitable for use as a concentrate for tie-dye on cotton, and acids on silk. If acid or reactive dyes are not available, other dyes can be used in the normal way, *provided that the string forming the resist is pulled tight enough* to withstand prolonged immersion in the dye. Any dye can be used as a concentrate, but few will prove wash fast. Domestic dyes are particularly useful here as they can be quickly mixed to a concentrate for use on small experimental samples, or fabrics that are not to be washed. Pigments can also prove successful when used as a 'paint' to emphasise or highlight small areas. Pigments do not penetrate many layers of fabric, unlike a liquid dye, but give a dense, solid coverage which is most effective along the edges of folds or pleats, making them more noticeable and giving them greater definition.

It is not advisable to use pigment on a fabric that is heavily creased or crumpled, as opposed to one that is methodically folded or pleated. The texture and appearance of pigment is so different from that of the dyes that if it is painted on to a densely compressed piece of dyed fabric, the patterns that it forms can look disjointed and unrelated when the fabric is opened out. Pigments should not be used unless the very obvious contrast between the dye and the pigment is actually required.

For dyeing and concentrate recipes see Chapter 6, pp. 151–63.

FABRICS

Fabrics such as fine cotton and silk are the most suitable for tie-dye. Bulky fabrics become extremely dense when crumpled or pleated, and are therefore difficult to dye.

However, some heavier fabrics such as cotton velvet take dye so beautifully that it is worth persevering to find the best ways of dyeing them (see Fig. 7.13).

Designs using such a heavy cloth must be planned carefully to ensure that the part that is eventually to be most visible comes into direct contact with the dye. It may be necessary to fold the sides of the cloth into the centre, arranging the cloth so that the middle is exposed on the outside. This area will then receive more dye, and will be the part that shows the strongest patterns.

An even wider coverage will be obtained if the fabric is wrapped around something else such as a piece of waste cloth prior to being tied. In this way the dye will reach a larger area of cloth, and will not have to penetrate so many layers.

Cotton lawn and other fine fabrics are particularly successful when tie-dyed (see Fig. 7.5). Light, dreamy effects can be produced that are very interesting when seen over other fabrics. Such fabrics can also be stiffened to make semi-transparent window blinds.

Densely woven fine mercerised cotton will show the tie-dye effects most clearly, and synthetics can also be tie-dyed *provided the right dye is used*. Well-worn pure cotton sheeting is useful for samples, and for finished work the most delicate and spectacular results will be achieved on silk. As usual, care must be taken to determine the exact composition of fabrics before dyeing.

EQUIPMENT

Various bowls and containers will be necessary, the size and type depending upon the work that is to be done. The fact that the fabric is greatly compressed when tie-dyed means that very large containers are seldom necessary.

Small glass heat-proof containers will be needed for the mixing and heating of dyes, and larger metal containers if quantities of hot dyes are to be used.

A thermometer is useful for mixing reactive dyes, and rubber gloves and overalls are always neccesary!

A small sharp pair of scissors is a vital piece of equipment, needed to cut the tightly bound cord that ties the fabric. Scissors will also be useful if used in the following way to protect the hands and avoid blisters when tying the cord: if one end of the cord is attached firmly to the closed scissors, the scissors can then be gripped, and the cord pulled tight without hurting the hands (a bar of wood could be used in

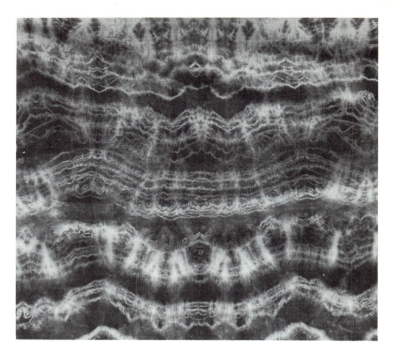

Fig. 7.5   Fine fabrics such as silk
are particularly successful when
tie-dyed

place of the scissors).

Sheets of polythene will be used to wrap up sections of cloth that are to be totally protected from the dye, and tough elastic bands will be needed to secure the polythene.

CORDS AND TYING THREADS

The fabric can be tied with a variety of threads, and experiment will show the thickness of line produced with each.

A strong button-hole thread will create a fine line, and string, linen twine, plastic-coated wire, and raffia can also be used to different effect. The most water-repellent thread is obviously the best choice, and experiments could be carried out with various waxed or coated garden twines.

A solid band of very tightly tied cord will resist the dye completely. After untying, it will result in a solid white stripe or a series of short irregular white bands against a darker background. If the dye has penetrated under the string, a jagged creeping line of colour will be visible on the fabric formed by the edge of the cord. This line of dye is normally paler than the background, giving a faded, or tonal effect. If the cord has been tied less regularly the white stripes or lines will be fragmented and will form broken bands of small criss-cross lines (see Fig. 7.5a).

TECHNIQUES

Methods of compressing and binding the fabric

The multicoloured effects that can be produced with tie-dye are achieved in basically the same way that they are with batik, using a resist (the cord) and dyeing from light to dark. The layer of binding tied around the fabric each time conserves the colour it covers by protecting it from the dye to be used next.

All the patterns on the fabric are made by compressing the cloth in one way or another, and then binding and dyeing it. The fabric can be screwed or crumpled, which produces random 'marbled' effects, or folded or pleated to create a more geometric layout. Figure 7.6 shows a variety of ways in which the fabric can be bound.

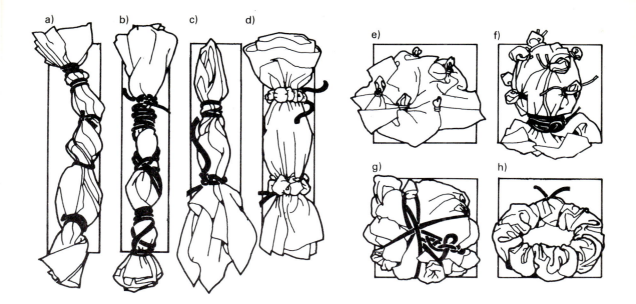

Fig. 7.6 Methods of binding the fabric.
(a) Pleated, twisted, and tied
(b) Tied with a criss-crossed cord
(c) Fabric picked up in a peak from the centre, and bound
(d) Channels sewn into the cloth have a cord threaded through, which is then pulled tight
(e) Small objects tied into the cloth
(f) Small objects tied into the cloth, which is then stretched over a large object and tied
(g) Marbling: the fabric is screwed up tightly and tied
(h) The fabric is rolled around a cord, tacked into place and the ends of the cord pulled up tightly

Tying objects into the fabric

Objects large and small can be tied into the cloth. They form circles, star shapes and rectangles, depending upon the shape of the object. The positioning of the binding, and the way in which the fabric is arranged over the object will also affect the results (see Figs. 7.1 and 7.2).

Small objects are most successful when grouped in one area, or enclosed within a specific shape. Massed patterns consisting of many tiny multicoloured rings can be built up by tying and dyeing areas that contain small stones or seeds, more seeds being tied into the cloth before each 'dip'. (Care should be taken to select objects that will not cook if a hot dye is being used!)

Large objects will form large shapes which could look ungainly, so it might be necessary to break these shapes up, either after dyeing, by overlaying them with pattern, or before dyeing, by screwing or tying the cloth before the large object is tied into it. Small objects could be tied into the cloth before the large one (see Fig. 7.6), or the cloth could also be gathered or pleated (see Fig. 7.7). Used with discretion, the method of tying objects into the fabric can produce interesting results; used without consideration, it is very difficult to avoid clichés.

Ruching

In this instance the fabric is rolled and tacked around a thick cord. When the two ends of the cord are tied together the fabric pulls up into tight gathers (see Fig. 7.6).

Alternatively, several channels can be sewn across the fabric and cord threaded through them. When the ends of the cord are tied together tightly the fabric pulls up into gathered lines.

If the areas of cloth that are to form the channels are large enough, small objects can be tied into them before the cord is threaded through. This will produce lines of small coloured patterns which are broken by the creases formed by the ruching (Fig. 7.6).

'Ruched' patterns are of great interest in furnishing and fashion as the fabric can be regathered after the cord has been removed, to hang in the folds created by the original ruching.

Ruching is also used with tri-tik, by gathering or tightly drawing up lines of small running stitches (see Fig. 7.4).

Pleating

Pleating is particularly successful with tie-dye. By continually pleating and dyeing a piece of fabric whole ranges of semi-geometric patterns such as tartans, checks, and chevrons can be produced (see Figs. 7.7 and 7.8).

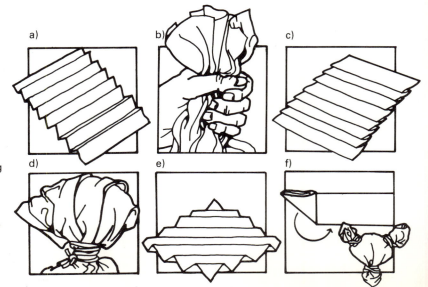

Fig. 7.7 Pleating and crumpling the fabric.
(a) Concertina pleating
(b) Crumpling freely
(c) Pleating
(d) Pleated and tied over a large object
(e) Diagonally pleated
(f) Pleated, folded, and tied at the corners

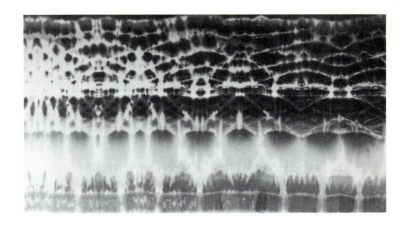

Fig. 7.8 Pleated and tie-dyed
fabric samples

These types of patterns can also be emphasised later. The fabric can be re-pressed to hang in the original pleats; it can be gathered, tucked, or pinch pleated and left to hang in soft folds. It can be lightly quilted, painted or stiffened, or worked on further with other resists.

If the fabric is not to have any practical use, but is intended to be purely decorative, it can be manipulated in many different ways to create a variety of three-dimensional effects.

Twisting

Twisting lengths of fabric, then binding and dyeing them produces random areas of colour and pattern that are particularly effective when over-dyed with other colours (see Fig. 7.9).

Before being twisted the fabric should be gathered, folded, or pleated into a narrow strip, and tied securely. With one person gripping each end of the cloth, it is twisted until it coils in half. The coiled cloth is then bound tightly. (One person can carry out the whole procedure alone by twisting the cloth over a door knob, or any other static object.)

When the dyed fabric is dry, it can be untied and the whole procedure commenced again, perhaps twisting the cloth at a different angle, and over-dyeing in another colour.

If desired, selected areas can be pulled up and tied before

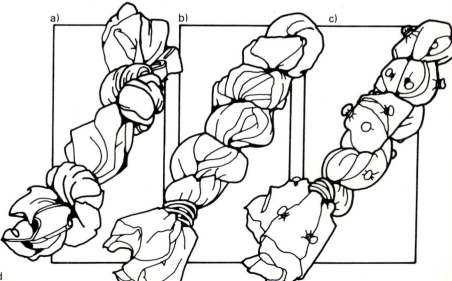

Fig. 7.9 Twisting:
(a) Twisted and knotted
(b) Twisted and coiled
(c) Twisted after having had small objects tied into the cloth

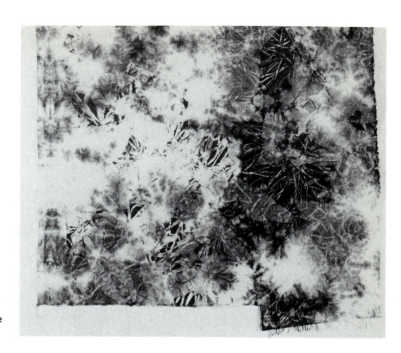

Fig. 7.10 Marbling. The fabric may have to be untied and re-dyed several times to obtain an even coverage of pattern. Sample by Julie Speechley

the length of cloth is twisted, or small objects can be tied into it prior to twisting.

When twisting the cloth it is important to do so very tightly and to secure it well to avoid large blank areas of colour that result from the total penetration of the dye.

Marbling

'Marbling' is a totally random effect caused by tying and dyeing a crumpled ball of cloth. (see Fig. 7.10 also 7.6 and 7.7) It may be necessary to tie and dye the cloth several times to obtain even coverage, as the density of the cloth prevents full penetration of the dye. If the fabric becomes very dense when compressed it can be crumpled around a waste piece of calico, or an object. This exposes more of the cloth to the dye, and gives a wider coverage of pattern (Fig. 7.10).

Characteristics of tie-dye, and how to control them

The type of shapes produced by tying and dyeing can be varied to some extent, but will always contain the bleeding and shaded effect that characterises the technique. This effect can be controlled to a greater or lesser degree, by: (a) the way in which the fabric is tied; (b) by dampening the fabric before dyeing it; or (c) by pre-treating some fabrics to be more resistant to particular dyes.

The colours of the work can be controlled to a greater extent. Traditional African tie-dyes consist of only two colours – the background colour and the dyed colour. Some Indian fabrics incorporate a third, or even a fourth colour, produced by over-dyeing. Whole ranges of vibrant and subtle colours can be produced in this way, and the muddy mixtures formed by dyeing unsuitable colours on top of each other can be avoided by the use of the resist, and by the technique of dip-dyeing, in which one part of the cloth is dipped into the dye, and other parts held clear. (see Figs. 7.11 and 7.12).

Fig. 7.11 Two colours can be simultaneously dyed, but kept separate from each other by binding

Fig. 7.12 Methods of holding parts of the cloth out of the dye.

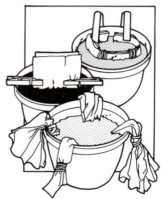

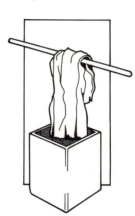

Fig. 7.11

Fig. 7.12

Dip-dyeing

The use of a dye concentrate is of particular interest in tie-dye. As it produces strong instant colour it can be used selectively in small areas without the dye bleeding excessively. This means that the fabric can be folded until very small, and the edges or corners can be dipped momentarily into the dye. Where the edges of the fabric touch the dye it bleeds slightly up the cloth, forming a soft dyed edge. A fabric that has been folded and dipped several times, when unfolded shows a kaleidoscopic pattern of colour.

As mentioned in Chapter 6, (pp. 159–62) there are several dyes that can be used as a concentrate provided that the fabric is treated afterwards to fix the dye. Procion M dyes are suitable for cotton fabrics, as are Dylon and other similar domestic dyes, and acid dyes for silk or wool. See Chapter 6 (pp. 159–62) for recipes.

Dip-dyeing with a concentrate is suitable for fine fabrics or where there are not too many layers for the dye to penetrate. When using thick or heavily compressed fabrics, normal immersion methods and recipes should be used as the dye will need more time to penetrate the fabric.

TIE-DYE: BASIC PROCEDURE

This will result in a multicoloured patterned sample.

(The same colour mixes can also be produced on pieces of cloth that have not been folded and tied, giving the coloured effects without the pattern formed by the cord.)

1. Bind the cloth tightly after having pleated, folded, or crumpled it. Criss-cross the cord if you wish, but do not entirely bind the cloth as space must be left for further tying.
2. Mix a pale-coloured dye. A greatly reduced primary would be a good choice as a wide range of colours can be dyed over it. Two different colours can be used on the same sample, one at each end. They can be allowed to blend in the middle, or can be kept separate by binding (see Fig. 7.11). The dye can be used hot or cold, as appropriate.
3. Dye, and dry the cloth. Do not untie it. If the sample has previously been pleated, the shapes made by the cord will open out to form a broken band when the fabric is unfolded. If it has been crumpled prior to tying, a more random pattern will result.
4. Add more binding to the cloth. If criss-cross areas of binding were previously applied, the patterns they will have formed can either be retained by protecting them with more string or polythene, or changed, by covering them with a further criss-cross layer of string that will create overlying lines of different colours. Tie, also, some of the plain dyed areas, leaving space for further bands of cord to be applied later.
5. Re-dye the cloth. Again, two separate colours can be used, or sections only can be dyed.

Remember, over-dyeing will give you the combination formed by one colour over another, for example a blue over a yellow will produce a green. If blue is wanted over a dyed yellow ground, parts of the string covering the white cloth should be untied, and the blue will 'take' as a blue on the white, and produce a green where it touches the yellow.

6. Continue tying and dyeing. The fabric may be untied at any stage, provided it is dry, or nearly dry. It can then be re-tied in a different way, and areas of it, or the whole of it re-dyed.

Normally, in dyeing, intermediate shades are made by dyeing one colour over another. Two colours are never mixed in solution and applied simultaneously. This is because different dyes 'take' on the cloth at different rates, and rarely colour a fabric equally if applied together.

However, in tie-dye, this characteristic can be exploited, as two colours which are applied when already mixed together will often separate at the edge of the resist. The dye which takes first forms a kind of coloured halo around the tied areas. This effect can be conserved during subsequent dyeing by covering the relevant areas with cord or polythene.

As well as samples experimenting with colour and over-dyeing, another range of small samples should be produced to show the results achieved by folding or compressing the fabric in different ways. If these are carried out in one colour only they will be more easily understood.

After the basic samples have been produced and the techniques understood, experiments can be carried out with less orthodox methods of tie-dye as given below.

PRODUCING SHARP, CLEARLY DEFINED PATTERNS

The bleeding effect that characterises tie-dye can be minimised in certain circumstances, and a much clearer line produced if required. This is usually done in conjunction with reactive dyes, due to certain characteristics of the dyes. Reactive dyes cannot tolerate acids, and so any fabric with an acid coating or content will resist the dye. So if parts of the fabric are dipped in an acid solution prior to dyeing with Procions, the Procion dye will only take on the areas that have not been in contact with the acid.

This is achieved in the following way:

1. Make up a solution of acetic acid and water, in the proportion of about 3 ml acetic acid to 1 litre of water.
2. Immerse the fabric in this solution, then take it out and wring it or squeeze it.
3. Prepare a solution consisting of 5 g or bicarbonate of soda in 1 litre of water.
4. Tie the fabric, and immerse it in this solution for a short while (2 minutes or so).

The soda solution neutralises the acid on the open (untied) areas, but cannot reach the acid-coated parts protected by the string. Any dye that subsequently seeps under the string will not take on these parts, and a clear delineation line will be seen.

Experiments could be carried out dipping parts of a sample into an acid solution and leaving parts untreated to compare results and to gain ideas that could be used on larger pieces.

Fig. 7.13 Dye-tie-dye. Velvet fabric sample, by Julia Lavis

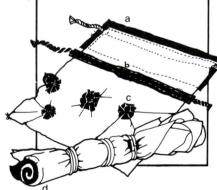

Fig.7.14 Colour transference:
(a) Strips of fabric sewn on to the back of the cloth
(b) Ribbon or tape used as a channel to hold cord
(c) Pieces of crêpe paper or tape tied on
(d) 'Swiss roll' of one coloured, and one white fabric
All the coloured fabrics should be non-colourfast in this instance

DYE TIE-DYE

Beautiful effects can result when cord which has been dyed with a non-colour-fast dye is used to tie the fabric (Fig. 7.13). This characteristic can be exploited in several different ways:

1. If the cord is still damp when the cloth is tied, the colour will transfer from the cord to the cloth. The tied fabric can be subsequently dyed in a lighter colour, and immersion in the hot dye will further release the colour in the cord.
2. The piece of cloth that is to be worked on can be wrapped around a waste piece that is either still damp after having been dyed, or that has been dyed with a non-fast concentrated dye. The two fabrics are then bound together, and some of the dye from the waste piece will transfer to the other, especially when forced to do so by the pressure of the string. The cloth can also then be dip-dyed in the normal way, and more colour from the waste piece will be released in the hot dye (see Fig. 7.14).

3. Small pieces of coloured tissue or crêpe paper (which are not colour fast) can be crumpled and tied into the cloth, or can be used to wrap objects that are to be tied into the cloth.
4. Coloured but non-fast strips of rag can be used to tie the cloth, or can be made to form channels to be gathered. Pieces of coloured cloth or paper can be used in this way with all tie-dye techniques to add another 'dimension' to the design. (Fig. 7.14).

Among the most interesting results achieved with this method are those where a wet dyed cord (it could have been previously dip-dyed in many colours) is used to bind an absorbent cloth such as velvet. No other dyeing technique is used in this case except the transference of the dye from the cord to the cloth. If many single layers of cord are used to criss-cross a gathered or pleated length of cloth the result will be a myriad of small lines in a multitude of colours (Fig. 7.13).

If such a thick fabric is pleated the dye will not penetrate all the pleats and will leave whole areas completely blank. Once this effect is known in advance, specific shapes can be pre-selected so that they form part of the design.

If piping cord has been used to tie the cloth, it will by now be multicoloured, and can be used to form parts of other designs in its own right by being fringed, plaited, or otherwise manipulated (see Fig. 7.15).

Fig. 7.15 Tassels and fringes made from dyed scraps of piping cord

DISCHARGE – TIE UN-DYE

Discharge methods are of particular interest in tie-dye as they produce a negative of the usual results (see Fig. 7.16).

With tie-dye discharge the fabric is dyed first. It is then tied, and soaked in a discharging agent. This leaves the dye underneath the string untouched, and so the result is a dark pattern on a lighter ground.

There are several methods of discharge dyeing, and many fabrics that have not been commercially dyed and fixed can be discharged.

The colour can be discharged in the following ways: (a) with bleach; (b) with dye remover available for use with

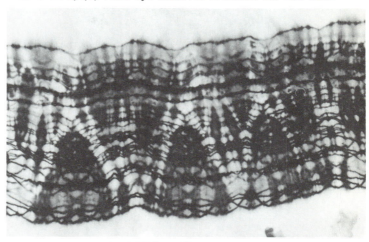

Fig. 7.16 Tie un-dye: dye discharged samples:
(a) On silk with a fine binding cord

(b) On cotton

Fig. 7.16   Tie un-dye: dye
discharge samples:
(c) On denim

domestic dyes; (c) by commercial preparations sold by dye
suppliers. For the use of all three methods see Chapter 6,
pp. 165–8.

Dye discharging is an intriguing technique. The stripping
agent might be expected to remove dye from the cloth,
exposing its original colour. In fact, this is rarely the case:
some colours discharge to a creamy colour; some to paler
versions of themselves, and some to different colours
altogether.

As with normal tie-dye methods the fabric can be dipped
and tied several times, producing different depths of colour.
The difference between tie-dyeing and tie-dye discharge is that
in one the colour is added on each 'dip' and in the other it is
taken away.

By combining both methods complex arrangements of
colour can be produced.

CHAPTER 8

Batik, wax resist, and starch resist

'Batik' is a word that describes a form of resist dyeing or printing. Batik fabrics are found in many parts of the world, but it is with Java that batik is generally associated.

Batik is an ancient craft, and one in which the basic techniques have changed little over the centuries. The resist, which is usually wax, starch, or resin, is stamped, stencilled, painted, or otherwise applied to the fabric. After the fabric has been dyed the resist is removed, leaving the parts of the fabric that were protected by the resist uncoloured. In the more complex batiks, several layers of resist and dye are applied, each resist protecting the colour it covers.

The various resist substances each have their own characteristics, and the one most commonly associated with batik is the crackled effect of wax. The cracks, which are deliberately allowed to form, enable the dye to penetrate, and leave a thread-work of fine dyed veins on the cloth.

There are also particular colours traditionally associated with batik, namely indigo (blue) and brown. The dye can be painted on, which gives the artist more control over which

Fig. 8.1 Batik garment piece from the Far East

colour goes where, or dyed on, in which case the fabric can be re-waxed and re-dyed several times to form a build-up of pattern and colour.

Batik cloth in Java was originally produced by the daughters of the upper classes, who had time to spare to perfect painstaking techniques. In Africa, batik is a village craft in which virtually the whole village participates. Recently, large textile factories have opened in Africa, and they use many different chemicals and techniques in the production of resist, and mock resist prints.

Mass production of textiles and pure native hand craft exist side by side in Africa; the traditional styles and patterns continue, and new ones come and go. The native techniques, however, change hardly at all, and give the fabrics a timeless quality: The original types of resist, and the same vegetable dyes are still used. The Yoruba people, who are famous for the art of adire (starch resist) are carrying on traditions that are many generations old.

Adire is a simple and direct technique that can create powerful and intricate results using the most basic materials.

Techniques for use in adire and batik are given below.

BATIK AND WAX RESIST

Batik is a very attractive craft to the amateur. It requires the minimum equipment, and that which is needed can often be adapted from household tools. Ordinary domestic dyes can be used, which are available in a wide range of colours, and are sold with any necessary additives. The stage-by-stage procedures are easy to follow, and once the resist process and the effects of dyeing colours over each other are understood, satisfactory results can be achieved relatively easily.

Anyone who has a small amount of space available in which to work, and some facility for heating wax and using dyes, is in a good position to experiment with batik. Even before using the resist a great deal can be learned from experimenting with dyes on a small scale to discover the (sometimes surprising) results that occur from dyeing and colour mixing (see Ch. 6, p. 162 and 163).

Fabrics

The selection of fabrics for batik work is influenced by several factors, the most important being the use of wax. Wax is usually applied hot to the fabric, and will bond to most fibres. When it cools, it forms the resist. If it is re-melted on the fabric (e.g. by hot dyes, or fan heaters) it liquefies and no longer acts as a resist. Therefore, it follows that cold dyes must be used.

Only certain dyes are suitable for use at low temperatures, and these include some domestic dyes, reactives, and acids (see Ch. 6.) Silk is the best fabric to use for batik if acid dyes are being used, and mercerised cotton will always give the best results with reactive dyes.

When choosing a fabric for batik, one of medium weight should be used, unless a large-capacity dye-bath is available, as the fabric must be able to move freely in the dye-bath.

Materials and equipment

Working surfaces
The fabric to be waxed is normally stapled, or otherwise fixed to a frame which holds it taut like a silk screen, and prevents the wax sticking the cloth to another surface.

Special adjustable frames can be bought, or old screen frames can be used. Purpose-built frames up to 3 m long can also be constructed, provided that storage space is available (see page 224). If a small frame is to be used, the fabric can be waxed in sections, although the constant removing and re-stapling of the cloth can prove tedious. If the wax is to be stamped on using a block of some kind, (see 'tjaps', p. 192) the fabric must rest on a solid, but soft surface. A table-top should be covered with a bed of newspapers. A sheet of heavy-duty polythene is then stretched tightly over the newspapers, and stapled to the table. This provides a firm surface on which to press the wax, and yet one from which the fabric can easily be removed.

The fabric to be worked on is taped to the table. Hot wax which penetrates the fabric will also hold it flat.

Dye vessels, heaters, and wax boilers
Vessels used for dyeing wax-covered fabrics must not be used for dyeing other fabrics. Pieces of wax, some so small as to be almost invisible, inevitably flake off the fabric during dyeing. No matter how well the pan is cleaned, these tiny spots of wax stick to its surface, and will flake off in the hot water used to dye the next fabric, causing indelible waxy marks. Incidentally, this also applies to tiny flakes of wax left on print tables. It is only too easy for wax to be ironed into a piece of fabric that is being laid down for printing.

If there is absolutely no chance of using separate pans for batik dyeing and ordinary dyeing, then the pans should be boiled out several times, and scrubbed, inside and out, with wire wool and an abrasive detergent (e.g. Vim) before any other dyeing is carried out.

Any container can be used for batik provided that the following points are observed: (a) it should be large enough for the fabric to be kept moving to avoid blotchy dyeing; (b) it should not be made of wood (e.g. barrels) as wood absorbs dye too readily; (c) chipped enamel containers should also be avoided for the same reason; (d) if plastic containers are used they should be *especially* well scrubbed after dyeing as anything that looks like a stain on plastic is actually surplus dye. Most dyes are originally pasted up in hot water, and some must be boiled, so a small heat-proof vessel and a source of heat will be needed. A large metal container will be necessary if residues of wax left in the fabric are to be boiled out.

The temperature of the wax should be carefully controlled and should not exceed 137 °C (280 °F). Below this the wax will not flow well, neither will it adhere to the fabric. Wax which is hot enough will nearly always be visible on the underside of the fabric. If it is not hot enough, it will simply rest on the top. Obviously, if the resist pattern is just on one side of the fabric, the dye can penetrate from the other.

Molten wax can be very dangerous and should never be left unattended. The ideal piece of equipment with which to melt wax is a thermostatically controlled double boiler, although the wax can, of course, be melted by other means. However, one precaution must be observed: wax must never be melted in a saucepan which is standing directly on the source of heat. Any metal container can be used to hold the wax, provided that it is standing in water, and that the water level is continually checked. (A characteristic hissing and crackling noise generally denotes that the water has boiled away – **fire follows**!)

Ordinary double boilers can be bought from hardware shops, or can be 'made' by standing a can, or cans of wax, in a saucepan of water. It is vital that the wax be kept close to the work, and a single hotplate is useful for this purpose, as it can be easily moved around. Any electrical extension leads must be either kept overhead or taped securely to the floor out of the way, to avoid tripping.

Tools

For the actual application of wax, any object can be used that will transfer the molten wax to the fabric. The traditional tools used in batik are the tjanting and the tjap (Figs 8.2 and 8.3).

Fig. 8.2 Tjantings and home-made tjaps

Fig. 8.3 A traditional Javanese tjap made of copper strips mounted onto wood

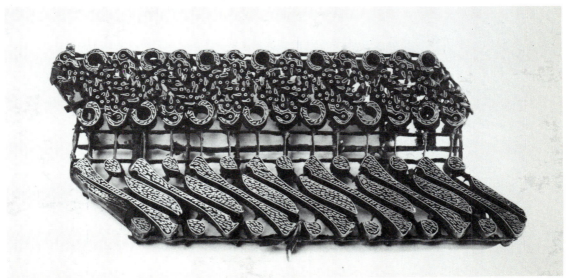

Fig. 8.4 Modern (Balinese) tjap printed and dyed fabric

The tjanting is a small cup made of metal (usually copper) which has a handle attached to it. The cup, which has one or more spouts, is filled with molten wax, which runs through it, enabling the tjanting to be used as a drawing instrument. Lines of various thicknesses can be produced by tjantings with different-sized spouts. Parallel lines are produced by tjantings which have more than one spout, and groups of dots can be made with multi-spouted tjantings. Electrically operated tjantings are also now available.

Tjaps were introduced to speed up the waxing process. They give a more mechanical look to the design, and enable the use of a repeat (Figs 8.4 and 8.5). A traditional tjap is made from strips of metal (usually copper) which are soldered together to form a 'printing' block. However, in the case of batik, the block is used to print a resist, not a colour.

'Tjaps' can be made from all kinds of found objects – nails, screws, bolts, raised metal grids, forks, pieces of pipe, metal cake rings and moulds. Small objects such as nails and screws will be easier to hold if fixed on to, or nailed into, a block of wood which is attached to a handle. This will also

Fig.8.5 Samples: patterns
stamped with home-made tjaps

protect the hands from the hot wax (see Fig. 8.2).

As hot wax quickly ruins brushes, a selection of cheap brushes should be set aside for batik. Wax-laden brushes can produce a wide variety of beautiful and simple marks. The shapes made can be varied by removing bristles, or by cutting them to different lengths. Samples can be produced on paper using different brushes, from large wallpaper paste brushes to small fine Chinese brushes. The mark made by each brush has its own intrinsic value, and a wide variety of designs can be made by using it.

Waxes

Two types of wax are used – paraffin wax and beeswax. Paraffin wax is hard, slightly fatty, and adhesive. It is paraffin wax that gives batik its 'crackle'. Beeswax is soft, and useful where a solid coating of wax is needed that will not crack. (It is also expensive!)

Beeswax and paraffin wax are normally mixed together in varying proportions, depending on the effect that is required. For normal work, a mixture of 70 per cent paraffin wax to 30 per cent beeswax is suitable. Wax is easily obtained in the form of candles, cakes of beeswax (from craft shops) and wax flakes.

Dyes

Cold-water dyes, (or at least those that react at a low temperature) are essential for batik. Domestic dyes such as Dylon cold dyes are a boon to the beginner, as they are easy to use, and are sold with the relevant fixing agents.

However, those planning to do any amount of dyeing, would do well to invest in a range of commercial dyes such as reactives or acids. Reactive dyes are eminently suited to batik as they must be used at low temperatures. Dyes such as those in the Procion M range can also be mixed to a concentrate for painting and spraying (see section on 'Dyeing with Procions' and 'Procion dye concentrate' (Ch. 6, pp. 157, 160). Acid dyes can also be used in this way (see Ch. 6, p. 155). Acid dye concentrate and Procion concentrate both require fixing.

When starting, it is wise to produce a range of basic samples. Pigments, water-colours and newsprint can be useful here, newsprint taking the place of the cloth, and pigment and water-colour painted on instead of dye. Working on newsprint will prevent you becoming too 'precious' about wasting cloth; you can make mistakes without worrying about the expense of the cloth!

Pigments, dyes, and waxes can all be used in different combinations on paper, as well as on cloth, to produce a rich variety of results. Colour mixing with pigments obviously does not produce the same results obtained when using dyes, but can at least give some idea of the batik process without the need to mix complicated recipes. Black pigment is also useful when used as a 'mask'. If the black pigment is painted directly onto the cloth, and the wax ironed off once the pigment is dry, the white spaces that are left can be coloured in many different ways. (For further use of black pigment, see 'Screen printing', p. 148 and 238.)

Techniques investigated on paper can often produce ideas for design on cloth, especially as the same media can be used on both.

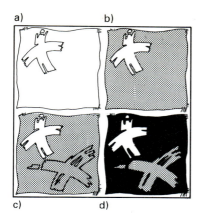

a)   b)

c)   d)

Fig. 8.6 The batik process.
(a) The first waxing
(b) The first dyeing
(c) The second waxing
(d) The second dyeing

Procedures

The actual procedures used in batik are easy to follow once several basic facts have been grasped.

1. The waxing process is one that reserves colour during subsequent over-dyeing (see Fig. 8.6).
2. The results of dyeing one colour over another are not always predictable, and some knowledge of colour mixing is necessary for this reason.
3. Batik is not a process by which quick results can be obtained, as the dyed fabric must be left to dry naturally. However, the clearly defined stages of batik mean that the work can be spread over a period of time.

It is worth while conducting experiments prior to, and during designs in progress. This will determine results in advance, and prevent mistakes occurring on an important piece of work.

Samples can be produced along the following lines:

1. Decide upon the base colour of the fabric (usually a pastel shade, or preferably, white.)
2. Apply the wax, making sure that it has penetrated to the underside of the fabric. If the wax is to be cracked, put the fabric in a cool place for a while before crumpling it.
3. When the wax is completely dry, dye the cloth following the recipe given with Dylon cold dye, or that outlined in Ch. 6, pp. 157–8. If silk, wool, or synthetics are being used, consult the relevant suppliers' instructions.

    For the first colour to be dyed, choose one which is closest in tone to the background colour. A pastel version of a primary colour is a good one to start with. This colour will influence all colours dyed over it, so choose carefully.
4. When the cloth has reached the required colour, remove it from the dye-bath, rinse and blot it well, and dry it away from direct heat. (If Procion dyes have been used, the fabric should be left to hang at room temperature for several hours or ironed, to fix the dye.)
5. Apply the second coat of wax, and redye the fabric in the second colour. Remember that this second coat of wax reserves every area of colour that it covers. Every part that is not covered with wax will be dyed in the second dye-bath.
6. When the second colour has been obtained, rinse, blot, and dry the cloth. (It is best to dry the cloth by hanging it in a warm room or by blowing cool air on to it with a fan or hair-dryer.)

    The sample so far consists of waxed shapes reserving: (a) areas of the base colour of the cloth; and (b) areas of the first dyeing (see Fig. 8.6). The unwaxed background colour is a combination of the first and second dyed colours.

7. Further waxing and dyeing can be carried out in the same way until the strongest colour is reached. As dyeing builds up, and the background becomes darker, the choice of colours to over-dye becomes more limited.

Remember that at any stage parts of the wax can be removed and the exposed areas of the cloth dyed in a colour that may not be compatible with the existing colours. For example, a sample has been dyed red. When dry, it is rewaxed and dyed green. The result is a piece of cloth coloured white (the background colour), red (the first dyeing), and *brown* (the combination of green over red). If *green* were wanted, some of the wax covering the white areas should be removed and the sample dyed green. The green dye would tint the brown darker, not affect the red (which is protected under the wax), but would dye the white green.

The intensity of colours that are dyed over each other is also important. In this particular sample, the wax could have been removed completely, and the whole sample dyed a very pale green (or any other pale colour): the pale green, in this case, would tint the white areas, but have little or no effect on the red or brown. Coloured backgrounds can be used to start with, but should be chosen very carefully, as the base colour, no matter how pale, can affect colours dyed over it. It is always wise to use white as a base colour as the results are more predictable. Mercerised cotton should be used to work on wherever possible to obtain maximum depth of colour.

Effects

Stippling, splashing, flicking, trailing; blobs, lines, and cracks. The marks made by the batik processes are so simple and strong that, when combined with the power and subtlety of dyes, they form shapes which are designs in their own right, and do not need to be formed into conscious imagery (Fig. 8.7).

Crackling

There are many commercially printed fabrics in the shops today loosely described as 'batiks' or 'batik style prints', on to which the 'crackle' has been printed by means of roller, screen, or heat transfer.

Where a true wax resist is used (e.g. in some commercially printed West African batiks) cracks are often

Fig. 8.7 Batik effects.
(a) Splattered wax
(b) Painted wax
(c) Lines drawn with a tjanting

produced by the ingenious method of pulling the length of waxed fabric through a small hole. This causes long cracks in the wax which, when dyed, create lines running parallel to the selvage.

When all the work is done by hand the cracking can be closely controlled. It can be placed deliberately, or allowed to form its own random pattern. Using different waxes, it can be made to occur wherever required. Cracks can be exaggerated, and checks formed by crumpling the cloth, or by folding it in different directions. The most noticeable cracks are made by chilling the waxed fabric before creasing it, either under cold water or in a refrigerator.

The crackle texture can be used in several different ways. It can form an all-over veiny pattern if used alone, or it can serve as a background texture for other designs. Veins of different colours can be dyed on the same piece of fabric in

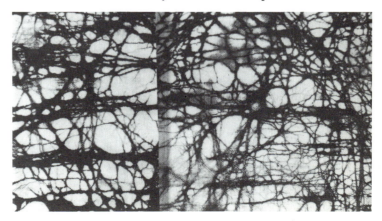

Fig. 8.8 The batik crackle

different ways: (a) By re-cracking the cloth after dyeing, and re-dyeing it. A paler or very different colour should be used in this instance, as a darker one will simply dye both the old cracks and the new ones, which will then appear to be the result of one dyeing only; (b) By removing all the wax, reapplying a new layer, and cracking it. This will form overlying cracks that can then be dyed in a darker or a paler colour; (c) By using concentrated dyes or print-paste, and sponging or painting different colours into the cracks.

Alternatively, cracking can be allowed to occur in one dyeing, and then covered with a second layer of wax to prevent colour penetrating the cracks during subsequent dyeing.

As well as being used as a pale background texture on top of which to work, the cracking can be used *on top* of designs, forming a network of veins through which the design is seen. This is achieved by removing all the wax once the work is complete, and replacing it with a thin layer of brittle wax that entirely covers the cloth. The wax is then cracked, and a concentrated dye mix is sponged over it, penetrating the cracks. Here, it is easier to use the concentrate than to try to immerse a stiff piece of cloth in a dye-bath. Also, there is less danger that the dye will bleed under the cracks. Pigment colours can be used for this purpose if they are well rubbed in. A colour should be chosen that is strong enough to have a noticeable effect over all the colours used previously.

This 'layering' of colours and shapes that occurs with batik should be clearly understood, as shapes which are applied last in wax, might be assumed to appear in front of others that they cover. In fact the reverse is the case: a shape which is applied in wax over another shape will always be seen

a)   b)   c)

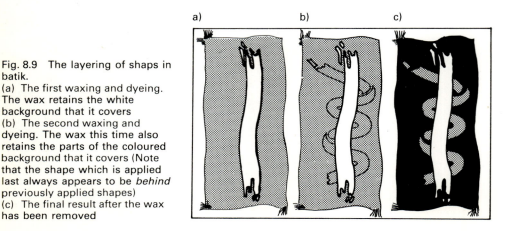

Fig. 8.9   The layering of shaps in batik.
(a) The first waxing and dyeing. The wax retains the white background that it covers
(b) The second waxing and dyeing. The wax this time also retains the parts of the coloured background that it covers (Note that the shape which is applied last always appears to be *behind* previously applied shapes)
(c) The final result after the wax has been removed

to be behind it, due to the fact that the whole of the first shape is already reserved under a layer of wax (see Fig. 8.9).

Splattering

The actual application of the wax can be carried out in several different ways. As well as being stamped on, or drawn on, it can be dribbled, or flicked on. This creates a splatter of tiny dots of wax which forms a pointillist effect. It is particularly successful when used in selected areas, or built up by rewaxing and redyeing, or when used as a fill-in to relieve flat areas of colour.

Blowing or flicking of wax can also be used in conjunction with a stencil. It is not advisable to paint solid areas of wax through a stencil (although stencils are used with starch resist) as a layer of wax quickly dries and tends to either fix the stencil to the cloth, or lift off the wax from the cloth around the edge of the stencilled shape when the stencil is removed.

When blowing or splattering wax, the instrument that is being used to apply the wax does not actually come into contact with the fabric. This, coupled with the tiny particles of wax, means that the wax is unlikely to penetrate the fabric. It is for this reason that splattering should be used in conjunction with hand painting, and not immersion dyeing, unless a very fine fabric is available.

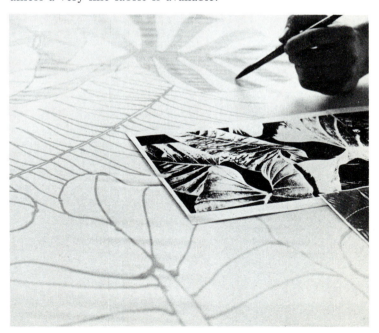

Fig. 8.10 Drawing with wax.
(a) Solid areas of wax are being filled in inside a waxed line

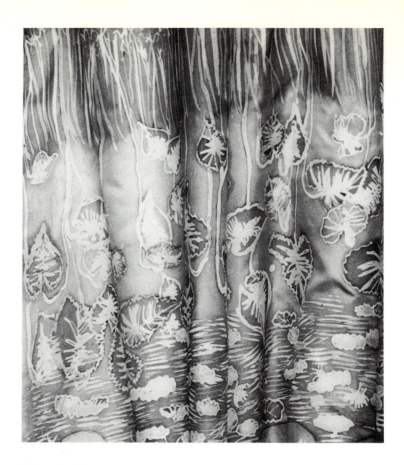

Fig.8.10   Drawing with wax.
(b) 'Lily-leaves'. Waxed and
painted design by Stella Davies

'Drawing'

The flowing quality of wax – especially when used with a tjanting – makes it an unusual and appealing medium with which to draw (see Fig. 8.10). As with pencil, the wax can be removed and worked over, yet the tjanting is really more like a pen, creating an even line that must be cross-hatched or scribbled to form tone. (A negative tone, as the lines remain white, being reserved under the wax.)

The effects produced with the tjanting are so seductive that they seem to bring out all the preconceptions and clichés that we have subconsciously absorbed, resulting in a wealth of multi-feathered birds, fire-breathing dragons, and stylized flowers. However, your personal experiments with other drawing media, and your observation of the way in which other artists have used line and form should (hopefully) equip you to use this medium to full and personal advantage.

WAX RESIST

Wax resist, in this instance, is the name given to a process whereby parts of the cloth are waxed (as in batik) and other parts are *painted* (see Fig. 8.11). The fabric is not immersed in a dye-bath. This difference is important for several reasons:

1. The dye mixture, when painted on, is more concentrated, and therefore requires careful fixing.
2. As the dye is applied to selected areas only, a wider range of colours can be used simultaneously without producing the muddy mixtures that can result from dyeing unsuitable colours over each other.
3. The actual colour mixtures produced are more easily

Fig. 8.11 'Hot bath', 95 × 121 cm by Noel Dyrenforth. In the collection of Professor Yoko Tajima, Tokyo

controlled as they can be mixed at source, and therefore it is not necessary to over-dye colours to create intermediate shades.

4. Subtle graded effects and tones can be introduced.
5. Pigment colours can be used.

With wax resist, the wax can be used to fulfil several different functions:

(a) It can prevent the dye from spreading too far, by forming the edges of shapes (Fig. 8.10).
(b) It can separate shapes so that different colours can be used adjacent to each other. (Fig. 8.10).
(c) It can be used as a 'painting' medium to create washes and layers of colour along with the dye (see Fig. 8.12).
(d) It can be used dry, in the form of rubbings taken directly on to the cloth.

Fig. 8.12 Wax can be used to create washes of tone and colour by being painted freely over previously coloured areas, which are then re-dyed

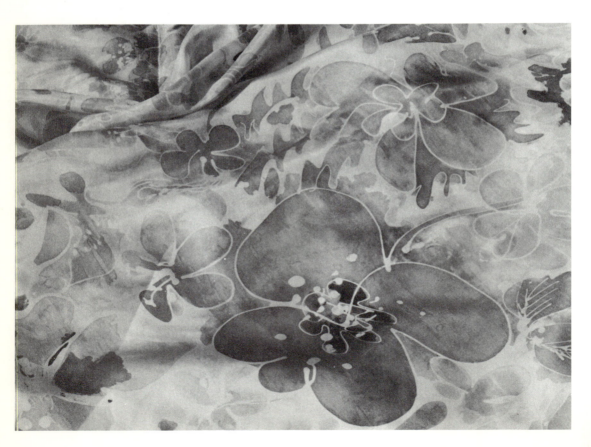

Effects and procedures

The effects produced with wax resist are different in many ways to those seen with batik, although the dye and wax can still be built up in layers if wanted.

Most of the techniques outlined in Chapter 9 can be used with wax resist. It is, however, not strictly necessary to thicken the dye, as the resist will prevent it spreading. The dye, therefore, can be used like water-colour. If a thick line of wax has penetrated the fabric. If a fine line of wax is all that painted onto the fabric. A tjanting line, however, is more vulnerable. Because of the fineness of the line, it should always be checked before painting to make sure that the wax is visible on the *underside* of the fabric, confirming that the wax has penetrated the fibric. If a fine line of wax is all that protects the edge of a shape, the dye should be painted to just within the edge of the shape, and allowed to bleed up to the wax. This will prevent the bleeding of surplus dye under the wax. Alternatively, the dye could be thickened.

Rubbings

Textures can be formed by taking rubbings directly on to the cloth with a candle. In true batik it is not advisable to use rubbings, whereas with wax resist, as dye does not actually *soak* the cloth, the wax, provided it is well rubbed in, will suffice to hold back the dye.

Coloured rubbings can also be taken using fabric crayons (see Ch. 9, p. 218).

Colour shading

Shaded water-colour effects can be produced within relatively small areas by laying on washes of colour, or by spraying with an air-brush. If the area is to be painted to form shading, the fabric should be dampened first, and the dye quickly washed over it. Concentrated colour can be built up in one part and faded into another. It is vital to work quickly to avoid visible lines. If a shape is to be shaded with a dark edge and a light centre, the fabric should be dampened to just within the waxed edge. When the dye is painted onto the dry area it will naturally bleed into the dampened part (see Fig. 8.13). A veined effect will occur if the dye is not washed and smoothed over the damp area.

If required, further colours can be added, before or after the fabric is dry. Many different colours can be painted within a waxed shape if a small brush is used, and the marks of the brush will always be diffused if the fabric is kept damp.

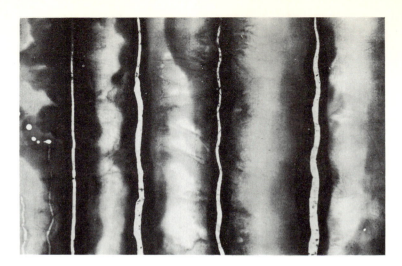

Fig. 8.13 Dye shaded up to a waxed edge

Cracking the wax

In batik, natural cracking occurs each time the fabric is handled. As in wax resist the fabric is not removed from the frame or the table until the work is complete, therefore the cracks must either be formed by using a brittle wax, or by removing the fabric from the frame, crumpling it, and then re-attaching it to the frame.

Dyes

A concentrated dye liquor or a pigment print-paste should be used with techniques that do not involve immersion dyeing. Thickened domestic dyes can be used, and Procions, mixed to the recipe given under 'Procion concentrate' (Ch. 6, p. 160), are highly suitable for cellulosic fibres, but will need to be fixed. Acid dyes can be used for painting on silk, and the maximum concentrate and minimum temperatures for their use should be checked with suppliers.

 The dye can be applied in any way that is practical, including spraying and painting.

Wax removal

Wax can be removed from the cloth by boiling, ironing, or dry-cleaning. Boiling is generally very messy, and it is preferable to boil out only the residues of wax that are left in the cloth after ironing, if dry-cleaning facilities are not available.

Removal of wax by ironing

Lay in a large store of newsprint or good-quality newspapers (the print will rub off cheap ones!).

Wax can be removed from the cloth by boiling or ironing.
1. Ensure that the dyed cloth is completely dry. Using a damp cloth, wipe off any dye that is left on the wax. This dye, if not removed, will iron through on to the cloth.
2. Crumple the fabric, and peel off as much wax as possible.
3. Cover the ironing surface with old newspapers. Lay the fabric on top, with one layer of newspaper or newsprint over it. (It is advisable to use white newsprint if possible, as the type on cheap newspaper tends to rub off, or transfer to the cloth).
4. Set an iron to 'hot' and quickly move it over the newspaper. The wax will immediately transfer to the paper. Remove the waxy paper, and replace it with new sheets. Iron the wax through, and then repeat the procedure with fresh sheets of newsprint until all the wax has been removed. Take care not to re-transfer any wax that is on the paper to the cloth.

Any slight greasiness left in the cloth can be removed by dry-cleaning.

Removal of surplus wax by dry-cleaning

By far the best way to remove moderate amounts of wax from dyed fabric is by dry-cleaning. After dry-cleaning the fabric feels as soft as it did originally, and the wax vanishes completely, leaving no haloing or greasy residue.

The dye should be totally dry and fixed, having been hung at room temperature for about 12 hours.

A cool rinse will wash away residues of dye. Many dry-cleaners will accept waxed fabric for cleaning, and self-service machines are often available.

If a large amount of wax has been used, most of it can be cracked and peeled, or ironed off before the fabric is cleaned.

If pigments have been used to colour the fabric it should not be dry-cleaned and one of the other methods should be used to remove the wax.

STARCH RESIST – ADIRE

The Yoruba people of Nigeria produce impressive fabrics using indigo dye and a starch resist paste made from cassava

Fig. 8.14 Nigerian adire cloth, on which the starch resist has been painted and 'combed'

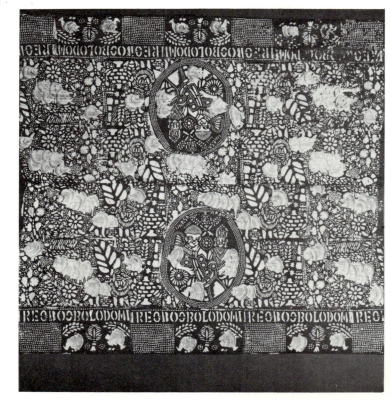

Fig. 8.15 Stencilled adire cloth showing swirling areas combed in the pools of paste

tubers (see Fig. 8.14). Traditionally these fabrics consist of two colours only, the white background colour and the indigo. The final depth of colour of the blue dye is determined by the amount of times the fabric is dyed. After as many as thirteen dyeings, the fabric is almost black, and the indigo, which is not highly rub-fast, comes off very easily onto the skin when the fabric is worn. This characteristic is considered highly desirable, and attempts to produce rub-fast indigo in the textile factories have been very unfavourably received.

The simplicity of the technique, combined with the power of the colour, makes these adire cloths very striking. Adire is similar to wax resist in some respects, as the best results are achieved when the dye is *painted* on, and does not fully penetrate the fabric.

Starch as a resist has different qualities from wax – some advantageous, some disadvantageous. Like wax it is used as a liquid, but as it does not dry so quickly, time can be spent considering its effects while it is actually being used. The obvious cracking seen in batik does not occur with adire, as the paste is more elastic. However, when the wet paste dries, it contracts and puckers the cloth. Cracks can be formed to some extent by gently pulling the cloth.

Two important effects which do characterise adire are produced using stencils and combs. Combs of different types and sizes can be used to create swirling patterns in the paste. Stencils are used to form a repeat in a similar way to that made by using a tjap, the wax being applied *on* the tjap; the paste *through* the stencil.

Tools and equipment

Stencils of various kinds can be used. Traditional stencils are cut from thin metal sheet. When parts of the stencil break away causing the paste to settle in large pools, the comb is used to break up the pools into swirling patterned areas (Fig. 8.15).

We are lucky to have a wide variety of materials from which to cut stencils. The most suitable are probably thin lino tiles or sheets of thin plastic. Card can be used, but has a tendency to become soggy after several applications of the resist.

Brushes and other applicators
When drawing delicate parts of a design, the native Nigerian craftsmen use a single chicken feather dipped in the starch. For larger coverage the paste is spooned on to the cloth and spread with the fingers. When we use adire techniques it is

not so easy to grab a passing chicken! In place of the chicken feather – or if an obliging butcher is not available to supply one – fine, old brushes can be used. Large ones are totally unsuitable, as the glutinous flour paste clogs them too quickly.

European and American craftsmen have experimented with other applicators (see Fig. 8.16). A tool used in the decoration of ceramics, known as a 'slip trailer', has been found to be useful. It consists of a rubber bulb with a rigid plastic nozzle attached. The bulb can be squeezed to suck up liquid, and squeezed again to release it. The liquid oozes out, forming lines. Squeezy detergent bottles and icing syringes can be used in the same way. A forcing bag can be made from a polythene bag with one corner cut off, the size of the hole determining the amount of paste that comes out.

'Combs' can also be made out of card, or teeth can be pulled out of plastic combs to give fine uneven swirls.

Designs can also be drawn into the pools of paste using a fine-pointed object such as a nail.

Fig. 8.16   Starch applicators

Pastes

Various recipes for the resist paste have been recommended. Some simply use flour and water, some cook the mixture, and some include starches or other substances.

Although experiments can be carried out to determine the perfect paste, an adequate paste can be made by simply mixing household flour with water.

The paste will have to be different thicknesses for different purposes. Obviously a paste which is too thick cannot be forced through a syringe, and one that is too thin will seep underneath a stencil. For general use, the paste should not be too runny, but should be thick enough to drop freely (like thick batter).

When making the paste, the water should be added to the flour slowly, to form a thick paste. Lumps must be dispersed, and more water added gradually. A blender can be used if available. The paste should then be cooked.

Fabrics

A fairly substantial cotton is normally used for adire, as the dye, which is *painted* on, must not be allowed to penetrate the cloth. Should the dye soak through the cloth to the underside, it would bleed back under the resist which just rests on the surface of the cloth, unlike a wax resist which seals the back as well as the front. Fine fabrics such as silk, are unsuitable, as they are easily penetrated, even by the thickest dye.

Dyes

Thickened domestic dyes and reactive dyes are the most suitable types of dye for use with a starch resist paste. If a purpose-built baker is available, pigments can be used. Reactive dyes are, as usual, the most successful, giving intensity of colour, and softness of handle (for recipes, see Ch. 6. pp. 159–60).

It should be borne in mind that any dye will penetrate the resist unless the resist is *totally dry*. Drying will take several hours.

Fixing the dye

Methods of fixing that involve the application of damp heat (such as steaming) will adversely affect the starch resist. Ironing is also sometimes impractical, owing to the thickness of the flour paste.

If pigments have been used they can be fixed by baking, as can Procions. However, although Procion-dyed fabrics can be baked in a domestic oven, pigment-coloured fabrics *must only be baked in a purpose-built baker*, as dangerous fumes are given off.

Domestic dyes often incorporate their own fixing agents, and do not require further fixing after dyeing.

Removing the resist

The flour paste should be carefully peeled and scraped off. It might be helpful to immerse the fabric in warm water while the resist is being removed.

Starch resist, although it seems a simple enough method to use, is surprisingly difficult to master. How much easier it would be if there was a cold resist paste that penetrated the fabric, forming a resist on both sides – one that would dry quickly, and be easy to apply! Well, fortunately, that possibility has now come about.

'GUTTA' RESIST

Gutta is a latex-derived resist which has recently become available from a limited number of suppliers. It takes the form of a thick, colourless, slightly rubbery liquid that will penetrate a fine fabric and stick to it, forming a resist which is soft and pliable even when dry. It can be painted on, or applied through a forcing bag or 'pipette' (sold through suppliers). It can – and should, in some instances – be thinned with a proprietary thinner, and in this form the finest of lines can be drawn with it which are nevertheless strong enough to act as a resist.

Gutta has several advantages over wax and starch resists: unlike wax resist it can used cold, yet, unlike starch resist it actually penetrates the cloth, forming a seal on both sides.

The gutta fluid can itself be coloured with any paint for which white spirit is the solvent. Gold, silver, and black gutta is sold by suppliers, and this can be used to form a deliberate outline to shapes that are part of the design and are not removed.

Dyes for use with gutta

Special alcohol/water-based dyes are recommended by suppliers for use with gutta resist. In practice, as most gutta work is done on silk or wool, Acid or Procion dyes can be used (for recipes Ch. 6, pp. 157–60). The choice of dyes is very important for several reasons: the gutta line, if it is fine, does not necessarily need to be removed; as it is so pliable it does not affect the feel of the cloth, with dyes such as Procions which can be fixed simply by air-hanging, the gutta line need not be affected at all. Acid dyes and the special recommended dyes (trade name: 'Super Tinfix') do, however, require steaming to fix them. This process might affect the gutta, making it stick to the paper that is used to roll the cloth in during printing. Should this happen, the gutta line can be removed permanently by soaking the fabric in white spirit, when the dye is fixed (see 'Fixing the dyes', below).

As this is a relatively new technique experiments should be carried out with different dyes and techniques, always with reference to the supplier's suggestions.

Characteristics and procedures

The fabric that is to be painted with gutta is usually fixed to a frame. This ensures that the gutta fully penetrates the cloth and does not stick it to a flat surface.

The consistency of the gutta is very important. It should be thin enough to penetrate the cloth, but enough to seal it and form a resist. If it is too thick however, it will rest on one side of the cloth only and, again, will not form the resist. If the gutta does prove to be too thick it can be diluted with pure surgical spirit (denatured alcohol) or the proprietary thinner sold by the suppliers. It should be diluted very slowly, drop by drop, to prevent it becoming too thin. The mixture should be tested on cloth while it is being diluted until a consistency is reached that is exactly right. The final mixture should have a consistency of thick single cream, or thin honey, and should dry on the cloth in about 10 minutes. If, during experiments, a gutta line does not hold back the dye it may be necessary to thicken it, or re-gutta over the gutta that can be seen on the back of the cloth. This sometimes occurs if a heavier fabric is being used. If, on the other hand, the gutta does not dry within 15 minutes, making it impossible even to apply the dye, this means that the gutta is too thick and should be removed. It can be removed by soaking the silk in *clean* white spirit. Small blobs of gutta can be removed by rubbing the silk between two pads of cotton wool, one soaked in white spirit, one dry. Like a wax line drawn with a tjanting, a gutta line tends to start and finish with a blob. This can be avoided by beginning the line on a piece of paper and drawing it off on to the work. If the pipette is lifted quickly at the end of the line no blobs should occur there either.

The gutta can even be screen printed on to silk, and by this method replicas can be produced. They can be painted or dyed in the same, or different colourways. As gutta is expensive this fact should be borne in mind when planning to print with it!

Fixing the dyes/removing the gutta

A fine gutta line does not necessarily need to be removed. As it is so pliable it does not affect the feel of the fabric and so can be left on it. Any larger lines that are required to be removed can be removed by soaking the cloth in white spirit *after* the dyes have been fixed. This should be done outdoors if possible to avoid inhaling fumes. The fabric can also be dry-cleaned. This removes any traces of the gutta.

Fixing of the chosen dyes should be carried out in the normal way as recommended by the suppliers. Samples should always be produced first to determine which dyes and fixing methods are most suitable for use with the gutta. If in doubt, stick to the supplier's instructions, using their recommended products and procedures.

CHAPTER 9

Hand painting

The hand painting of fabrics is an ancient craft, examples of which have been found that date back as early as 4,000 years BC.

Today, the techniques that are used for painting on cloth are so many and varied that the scope and type of work produced is limited only by the imagination. The scale can be enormous – literally – as lengths and widths of cloth can be joined together *ad infinitum* to increase the size of the original piece.

Fabric can be coloured with any medium that will adhere to it, the only consideration being the final use of the cloth, and whether it will need to be washed or dry-cleaned. Careful planning is necessary when mixing media on one piece of work as some media require fixing, some are not suitable for dry-cleaning, some are not wash-fast, etc.

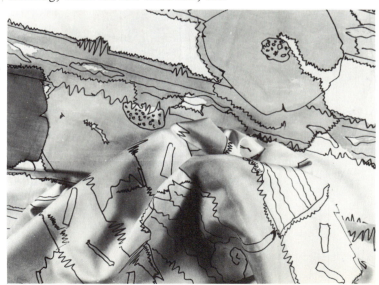

Fig. 9.1 Hand-drawn and painted fabric by Andrea Thompson

Many media that are normally used on other surfaces have, in practice, been found to be successful when used on fabric. These include some felt-tipped pens, special ball-point pens and spray guns, and are listed under the headings given below.

PAINTS

The term 'hand painting' when applied to textile crafts usually involves the use of dyes, as, by their nature fabrics are assumed to have a practical function and most dyes are wash-fast when used on a suitable fabric.

However, if the fabric is not intended to be washed, many different media can be used on it, and paints are the obvious choice. (Our art galleries are full of hand-painted canvases, after all!) The important thing is to understand the characteristics and limitations of the medium that is being used. Although some paints can be made to resemble dyes, they cannot be truly used as dyes, not being wash-fast. Instead of using paint to imitate dye it should be used in its own right, and its own special characteristics exploited.

Different types of paint obviously have different appearances: some gloss paints and enamels form a hard shiny surface against which softer effects can be set. Some plastic-based paints such as acrylics can be almost 'sculpted' to form raised surfaces. Emulsion paints can be used like pigments or gouache, and can even be printed. (White emulsion can be especially useful when used like white pigment as a cover for mistakes!) Many paints can be sprayed through a spray gun provided that the relevant solvent is available for cleaning the equipment.

Oil paint, water-colours, acrylics, domestic and industrial paints: there will be a surface and a circumstance to suit each of these.

BALL-POINT FABRIC PENS

Ball-point fabric pens are now readily available. Such pens consist of a tube (rather like a toothpaste tube) with a nozzle at one end which contains the ball tip. A gentle pressure on the tube forces out a thick colour which is similar in consistency to pigment print-paste or thick gouache. This type of pen is ideal for line work, or for small areas of colour,

Fig. 9.2 A ball-point fabric pen being used to outline a screen print. Design by Jayne Howlett

where it can be used in place of screen printing. However, over a solid area larger than about 8 cm in diameter the colour can look and feel very heavy and solid, so the use of the pen is limited in this respect.

The colour range of fabric pens is wide, and includes metallic silvers and golds, fluorescent, and pearlised colours. The metallic colours have a surface which is slightly rough, like Lurex, and the pearlisers, which are semi-transparent, are laid over certain other colours to give them a lustrous sheen.

The pen is used like an ordinary felt-tipped pen, moved to and fro until an even coverage is obtained. Special metal frames are sold for use with the pens, and these enable a small amount of cloth at a time to be held taut in contact with a flat base. However, if a large piece of cloth is being used, it is more practical to tape or pin the whole piece of fabric to a print table or other flat surface.

Fabric coloured with fabric pens is wash-fast, and the pens can be used on many different fabrics (see suppliers' instructions).

The effect of these pens is best demonstrated in conjunction with other media, where their drawbacks are not so obvious, and their advantages can be fully exploited (see Fig. 9.2).

FELT-TIPPED MARKERS

Graphic designers are familiar with the enormous range of felt- and fibre-tipped markers available for use on paper. These pens come in a bewildering variety of shapes, sizes, and colours, but generally speaking, fall into one of two categories: oil-based and water-based. Water-based pens can be used like water-colour paints – diluted and made to form washes. They are not permanent on fabric. However, pens marked 'permanent' or 'waterproof' will often be found to be wash-proof when used on fabric, and tests carried out on various fabrics will show which are most suitable for use with particular markers.

Before a whole range is bought, pens of different makes should be tried out on samples of cloth to discover whether or not they are wash-fast. They may prove to be fast through two or three washes, or may last considerably longer. They may, however, be found not to be dry-cleanable, or light-fast. Producing a range of samples will, as usual, reveal all.

All the samples should be produced on *white* cloth. Simple marks and lines should be made on the cloth, after which it should be dried thoroughly, and washed and rubbed well with detergent. Some colours will run and stain the cloth – and may form interesting effects in their own right. Those which do not run should be noted, as other colours in the same range are also likely to be wash-fast.

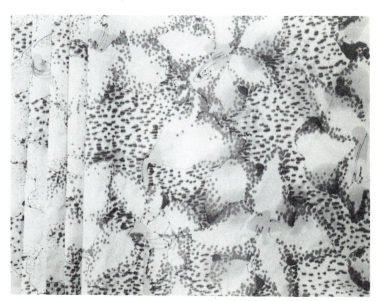

Fig. 9.3 'Lilies', by Alison Hesketh, drawn with felt-tipped pens on silk. Note the characteristic bleeding effect

The colour might also bleed while it is being applied. Liquid media always bleed on cloth to some extent, especially on silk, and this characteristic can be emphasised by using fabrics with a distinct weave, such as twill, as the colour will spread along the lines of the weave.

If the colour does run it will probably form a shaded effect, fading in intensity from the solid area of colour. This effect can be accentuated if required by dampening the fabric first – with water, or a relevant solvent. A line that has bled can create a 'neon' effect if it shines out from a dark ground. This is achieved by painting over the line with a wax resist that covers both the painted line and a small part of the background along it. If the cloth is subsequently dyed in a dark colour the painted line will shine out from the background once the wax has been removed.

Whole lengths of fabric can be drawn and coloured freely with felt markers, and they are especially useful where a fine outline is needed. Fine lines are difficult to produce on a screen unless a good vacuum is available during exposure. Such lines also tend to block during printing, so in some cases a pen line is more practical, especially where a spontaneous non-repeating design is being produced (see Figs. 8.12 and 9.3). Drawings done on cloth with a fine-nibbed pen can look impressive when combined with washes of colour and delicate hand stitchery.

CRAYONS

A crayon texture can be used to break up large flat areas of colour, or to create texture for its own sake. It can be produced on cloth in several ways, as follows:
1. By taking a crayon rubbing onto Kodatrace and exposing it onto a screen (see Fig. 5.14).
2. By drawing directly onto the cloth with special fabric crayons (see Fig. 9.4).
3. By means of heat transfer, which transfers the crayoned colour from paper to cloth by the application of heat (see Fig. 9.5).

The method of crayoning onto Kodatrace is outlined in Chapter 5 (pp. 94–5). Once on the screen the crayoned texture can be printed onto any fabric, provided that a suitable print-paste is used.

Several types of fabric crayons are available today, and care should be taken to choose the right type for a particular purpose, as some crayons are suitable only for use on

Fig. 9.4 Fabric crayons used on silk in conjunction with a screen print. The textured crayon effect is produced by rubbing on the fabric over a textured surface

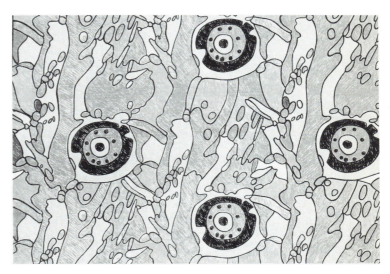

Fig. 9.5 Heat-transfer crayon used over a screen-printed line

synthetics, and others for natural fibres.

Generally, heat-transfer crayons are suitable only for synthetics: Crimplene, Tricel, Trevira, and most nylons. The original design that is to be transferred to cloth is drawn onto paper. This is then placed face down on the cloth. The heat from an iron (or a special heat-transfer bed) transfers the design to the cloth. The paper design can be used several times, the colours becoming less intense each time. This method, in its

Fig. 9.6 An industrial heat-transfer machine. The patterned paper can be seen feeding into the machine where it is held in contact under heat against plain cloth. The pattern transfers to the cloth

Fig. 9.7 A range of samples produced by Storey's Decorative Products, showing the variety of effects that can be produced by heat transfer

most sophisticated form, is used a great deal in the textile printing industry today, the design being printed onto large rolls of paper with heat-transfer dyes, and later transferred to cloth (see Figs 9.6 and 9.7).

The wax from heat-transfer crayons can be applied to the transfer paper in many ways apart from the more obvious ones. It can be melted into blobs and dropped on, or the crayon can be scraped and the slivers of wax fused together between two sheets of paper with an iron, the mottled effects being subsequently transferred to the fabric.

The appearance of heat-transfer crayons on fabric is similar to that of dyes, as they do not form a thick surface layer, but seem to be part of the cloth. They are particularly versatile in that random textures made on paper can be cut into hard-edged shapes which can then be transferred to the cloth, maintaining the soft effect, and the hard edge.

Heat-transfer crayons are available from craft shops, and transfer *dyes* and small heat-transfer presses from specialist suppliers.

Direct fabric crayons are extremely versatile. They are great fun to use, and surprisingly sophisticated results can be achieved with them.

Many different effects can be produced with fabric crayons, among the most successful being rubbings (see Fig. 9.4). Rubbings from any raised and textured surface can be taken directly onto a medium-weight or (preferably) fine cloth. Being waxy, the crayons form a permanent resist to water-based media, and liquids such as dyes or pigments can be used over, and in conjunction with them, and will colour the parts of the cloth that are not already covered with crayon. (surplus blobs of dye should be wiped off the crayon). When this technique is used with wax resist, the candle wax which forms the resist is removed when the dye is dry. When the resist is formed by fabric crayons the coloured crayon is an integral part of the design, and is not removed.

Although the colour range of direct fabric crayons is somewhat limited, the fact that colours can be overlaid and blended to some degree means that the range can be increased.

DYES AND PIGMENTS

The bleeding that occurs with dyes when they are painted on-to cloth can be exploited as a positive feature, or controlled,

Fig. 9.8 Painting with dyes and pigments over a fabric pen line. Design by Andrea Thompson

using resists and thickeners. Different liquids spread on fabric to different degrees in any case, and often this characteristic is part of their attraction.

Most commonly used for printing and painting on fabrics are dyes and pigments, and the differences between the two become most apparent when they are used for painting. Pigments are related to paints; they spread very slowly, giving a firm edge to shapes without excessive bleeding. Like gouache, they have a matt surface. Their main drawback is that they can prove rather stiff if used in overlays over a large area. It is for this reason that dyes are to be preferred for hand painting wherever possible.

Most dyes can be painted on to their compatible fabrics, either as a concentrate, (not all dyes are recommended for use as a concentrate: check with suppliers) or in a solution of a normal strength. If dyes are used at normal strength for painting, repeated applications will be needed to bring the intensity of the colour up to that of a concentrate.

Small test-pieces can (and should) be produced to test colour and wash fastness.

THICKENERS

When dyes are used for printing they are thickened with gum to make a more manageable medium that does not bleed on the cloth. If the amount of thickener is reduced, an ideal painting medium results.

Domestic dyes such as Dylon can be thickened by the addition of Paintex, and dyes such as reactives and acids can be thickened by adding them to the relevant thickeners. When the colour has been fixed, and the fabric washed, the gum disperses, leaving the fabric soft.

Pigments, being a relatively thick liquid in any case, are suitable for painting in the form that they are sold, mixed with the relevant binder.

Commercial dye thickeners generally fall into one of the following categories:

1. Sodium alginate thickeners of which Manutex is one.
2. Carboxy methyl cellulose thickeners, of which Solvitose is one.
3. Modified starch-based thickeners, of which Thickening 301 is one.

Each type of dye is used with its appropriate thickener. However, in practice it is found that Thickening 301 can be used to thicken most dyes, enabling them to be printed and painted.

A high-speed mixer is useful when mixing thickeners, as they are often sold in powder form, and must be thoroughly mixed with water.

Directions for mixing thickeners can be obtained from suppliers. Manutex, listed below, can be used with Procions and acid dyes.

The following recipe produces a Procion *print*-paste. An easier painting medium can be produced by reducing the amount of thickener.

Printing and painting recipe for Procion M dyes
You will need:

10	parts	urea (grams)
46.5–42.5	parts	water (millilitres)
1–5	parts	Procion M dyestuff (the amount of 'parts' depending upon the depth of shade required)
40	parts	Manutex RS 5% thickening
1	part	Resist Salt L
1.5	parts	sodium bicarbonate
100	parts	

(All 'parts' are grams if dry weight, millilitres if liquid weight.)

The Manutex RS 5% thickener is mixed as follows:
1. Take 1 part Calgon dissolved into 14 parts water at 40 °C (104 °F). If hotter water is needed to dissolve it, allow it to cool to this temperature.
2. Add 80 parts cold water.
3. Sprinkle 5 parts Manutex RS 5% on to this solution and stir for 5–10 minutes. Disperse any lumps.

The dye solution is mixed as follows:
1. Put a little of the water aside for the sodium bicarbonate. Dissolve the urea in the remaining water, the temperature of which must not exceed 70 °C (158 °F). Allow it to cool to 50 °C (122 °F).
2. Use this solution to paste up and dissolve the Procion M dyestuff (strain it through gauze if necessary).

The print or paint paste is mixed as follows:
1. Take the dye solution and stir it well into the thickener.
2. Add the Resist Salt L.
3. Just prior to printing, the sodium bicarbonate, dissolved in

a very little amount of *warm* water is stirred in. **Do not** use hot water.

Once the sodium bicarbonate has been added the paste is usable for only 1–2 hours, so the paste and bicarbonate solution should be kept apart until needed, or added together in proportionate amounts as work progresses.

Some Procion M dyes are suitable for use on silk. However, it should be noted that if the alkali used with Procions (sodium carbonate or sodium bicarbonate) is too concentrated it will rot the silk. So, if Procions are being used on silk, an addition of acid could be tried in place of the alkali. Not more than 2 per cent (2 parts per 100 of water).

Acid dyes thickened to use for painting

An acid concentrate, thickened for painting on silk and wool, can be prepared by following the recipe for acid concentrate given in Chapter 6, and adding the dye solution to a suitable thickener. Such thickeners include 'Thickening 301' (manufacturer: Grunau) and Manutex RS 5%. (See UK suppliers, p. 240 for both of these products).

As Thickening 301 has been found to be suitable for thickening most dyestuffs for printing and painting, it would be useful as a general all-purpose thickener.

Many dyes require fixing after use, and dye concentrates especially should be fixed thoroughly. Methods for fixing are outlined in Chapter 6, pp. 160–2 and should be studied carefully.

Recipes for painting other fabrics such as synthetics can sometimes be obtained from relevant suppliers where their produce is suitable for this purpose. Details of fixing, where necessary should also be obtained from suppliers.

WORKING SURFACES

For painting, the fabric is normally either stretched across a frame (see Fig. 9.8), which allows the dye to spread and dry freely, or fixed to a print table. If the latter method is used, it is advisable to keep a back-cloth underneath the fabric, as dye which penetrates to a rubber surface quickly bleeds back into the painted cloth, where it spreads excessively. It also dries, leaving noticeable water marks in the painted areas, and unwanted rings of colour that have spread across the unpainted areas.

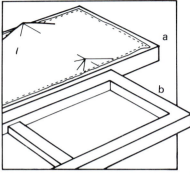

Fig. 9.9 Stretching the fabric over a frame avoids patchy areas. (a) Use of a 'tent-pole' to raise the fabric above a centre strut. (b) A frame where the centre strut is set lower than the rest of the frame

Likewise, if a frame has been used, designs should be planned that do not include the edges of the cloth that are resting on the frame, as any painted area that rests on another surface will show water marks and patchy colour.

If a long length of fabric is being painted on a frame it is likely that the frame will have a centre strut. In this case the fabric must always be held above the strut and must not be painted while resting on it, or allowed to rest on it while still damp. This can be avoided by using a short, thin, pointed object as a 'tent peg' to stand on the centre strut and hold the fabric away from it in a peak (see Fig. 9.9).

If a frame is to be purpose-built the centre strut can be set lower than the rest of the frame so that even if the fabric sags slightly it will not rest on the strut (see Fig. 9.9).

When the fabric is fixed to the frame it should be pulled just taut enough to hold it flat, yet not so tight that it pulls in grooves across the frame. It is important to keep the tension equal over the frame as dye will collect in any tiny channels on the cloth.

FABRICS

Any fabric is suitable for hand painting so long as it has an affinity with the dye being used. If the fabric is not to be washed, this point will not be so important.

When a fabric is immersion dyed the whole cloth is immediately covered in dye, and so it is not possible to see how the dye actually covers the cloth. When dip-dyeing or hand painting, the way in which the dye creeps along the weave of the cloth is more obvious. Experiments with blobs of dye painted on to differently woven surfaces will show that dyes bleed into horizontal or diagonal lines on some fabrics, and bleed outwards, forming uniform shapes, on others.

Hand painting of the most decorative kind is usually done on silk, satin, or thin cotton, as the fluidity of the dyes seems most suited to these delicate materials. Silks are of particular interest when experimenting with dyes, as the differently woven silks are clearly distinguishable and it is therefore easy to note how the dye spreads over them. Silks which have a slub will often show fine dark lines when dyed, due to the slub thread which absorbs more dye. The dye will spread evenly along the threads of a coarse but evenly woven silk, also emphasising the weave. Some silks are very easy to fray, and multicoloured fringes and dyed tassels can be created by using them (Fig. 9.10).

Fig. 9.10 Multicoloured fringes
made from frayed painted stripes

The variety of fabric surfaces is enormous, and all can be painted, with different results. Fine gauzes can be used to cover other fabrics; heavy cottons can be painted and quilted. Fabrics such as velvet can be shaved and have colour painted on to the weave; long pile fur fabrics can have dye applied to the ends of the pile; and plasticised fabrics can be painted with oil-based inks. The list is endless.

PREPARATION OF FABRIC FOR PAINTING

Fabrics unprepared for painting should be scored following instructions given in Chapter 6, p. 153–4.
If unthickened dyes are being used on silk without a resist, the silk can be treated prior to painting, to prevent excessive dye bleeding:

1. Dissolve 250 g of cooking salt in 1 litre of water.
2. After 1 hour filter the water through a fine sieve, muslin, or a filter coffee paper.
3. Soak the silk in the mixture, and hang it out to dry.

226

HAND PAINTING: EFFECTS AND PROCEDURES

If dyes are used, they should be treated like water-colours. Flat, even colour is difficult to produce when painting with dyes, which naturally run and overlap, forming washes of colour and overlays of tones and shades.

Although brushes are the obvious tool with which to work, with a little imagination the dye can be applied to the cloth using any instrument that seems suitable at the time. Sponges, wads of cotton wool, and paint rollers can all be used to different effect.

A wide variety of brushes should be kept to hand, as each will be suitable for a different purpose. The dye can also be sprayed on (see 'air-brushes and spray guns', below). Thickened dye can be stamped on, using all manner of objects as 'printing' blocks.

The transparent wash of colour produced with dyes is the most easily recognised characteristic of hand painting. Washes can be created by spraying, or by painting onto damp cloth.

Obviously, the strongest concentration will occur where the cloth is driest, so it follows that if a fabric is progressively dampened, the intensity of the colour will fade from the strongest on the dry areas, to the palest on the most damp areas. If a fading area of colour is required the cloth should be dampened accordingly. Working quickly the dye is sponged or painted onto the driest area so that it begins to spread into the damp area. The dye must be sponged quickly to and fro so that no hard lines are visible.

Two different colours can be merged in the same way, one being worked up from the bottom, the other down from the top. Rainbow effects can also be created by blending whole groups of colours together, sponging or painting them onto a damp ground.

Complete lengths of fabric can be coloured in this way, using a sponge, paintbrush, or large roller.

Several things should be borne in mind while shading or blending colours by this method. It is important: (a) to work quickly to avoid lines forming; (b) not actually to *soak* the cloth, or pools of colour will collect in the sodden areas.

Experiment will show the degree to which dye will spread on different damp surfaces, and how far it can be controlled.

Unusual textural effects can also be produced by sprinkling salt crystals on to dye which is still wet. The salt crystals absorb some of the dye, and the remainder dries leaving a mottled pattern. Blobs of water, and pure alcohol (surgical spirit) have the same effect when dropped into wet dye. If even-sized blobs are wanted they can be dropped on

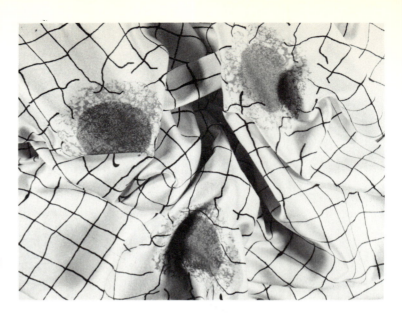

Fig. 9.11 Thickened dye stamped on with a sponge, used with a screen-printed line. Design by Winnie Kwan

through an eye-dropper, otherwise the spirit can be flicked on to produce a more random texture.

A pointillist effect can be made on a damp or a dry ground, using a very fine brush to dot colours over each other (this effect can also be produced using a splatter cap on a spray gun). The dots of colour will mottle on a damp ground, and form sharp dots on a dry one.

Sponges can be used to create a dappled effect over a background, or they can be used as a soft printing block cut into repeatable shapes. They can also be used in conjunction with a stencil to form localised texture (Fig. 9.11).

Another type of texture can be formed by flicking colour onto the cloth. If an old toothbrush is loaded with thickened dye or pigment the dye can be flicked off onto the cloth by running a thumb or knife across the bristles (see Fig. 9.12). This can produce a delicate and subtle texture, especially if layers of colour are built up.

A similar but coarser texture can be made by dabbing a stiff stencil brush onto the fabric.

Colour can also be blown onto the cloth through a diffuser, plant spray, or air-brush. Some of these give a fine spray, others a coarse one. Many plant sprays have nozzles that can be opened or closed to adjust the force and density of the spray (Fig. 9.13).

The most sophisticated method of blowing dye onto the cloth is by use of an air-brush.

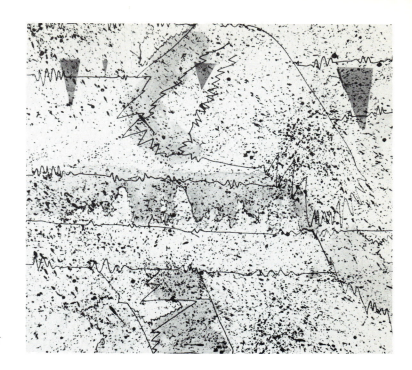

Fig. 9.12 Colour flicked on over a pen-drawn line

Fig. 9.13 Spraying: most suitable tools are the aerosol spray can (usually cellulose-or spirit-based paints), the spray gun, the air-brush, various plant sprays, and the diffuser

AIR-BRUSHES AND SPRAY GUNS

Air-brushing is an ancient art, dating back to prehistory and the caves of Lascaux and Pêche-Merle in south-western France. The 'negative hands' seen there on the cave walls were produced by a dye or pigment that was blown by mouth onto the rock, using the hand as a 'mask'.

The air-brush as such, became popular much more recently with the development of photography, when the fineness of the spray made the air-brush the ideal retouching tool.

The full potential of the air-brush as a graphic design instrument was quickly appreciated, and it came increasingly to be used for advertising and propaganda purposes. As technical virtuosity increased, air-brush designs became more and more sophisticated, until today, when artists produce astounding images of hyper-realism and fantasy.

One of the characteristics of the air-brush is that colours and shapes are built up layer upon layer using transparent 'washes' of colour. The transparency, liquidity, and brilliance of dyes make them ideal for use with an air-brush, and they are being used more and more by illustrators.

The fabric designer uses the air-brush in exactly the same way as the illustrator, except that the images and effects are built up on cloth, the end use of the fabric dictating the type of design that is produced on it. Air-brushed fabrics are completely wash-fast once they have been fixed, and can then be treated like any printed fabric (Fig. 9.14).

Spray guns are more likely to be used by the fabric craftsman than the illustrator, because of the wide coverage of the spray. Spray guns can be obtained in a variety of sizes, each designed for a specific purpose. They are powered by a compressor. Large spray guns, of the type normally used to spray vehicles, are attached to a container with a capacity of up to 1 litre. This type of spray gun has a large nozzle that can be opened up to produce a spray sufficient to cover a broad area with a dense liquid (e.g. spirit-based paints).

When used over small areas of fabric the effect of the spray is coarse, and gives a stippled effect, although when used on its intended scale it gives good coverage.

Smaller spray guns have a container that holds up to approximately $\frac{1}{4}$ litre of the liquid. The spraying range is less than that of the large guns, but the spray itself is finer, and the nozzle can be closed down to produce a very fine spray or line for close work. By replacing the normal nozzle cap with a splatter cap a spray can be produced that spits colour out irregularly, forming a speckled effect. This can look very

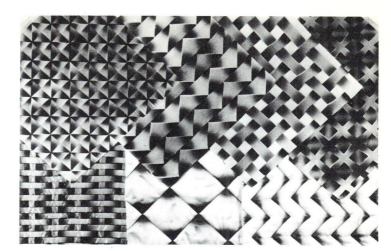

Fig. 9.14 (a) Small air-brushed samples by Diana Harrison

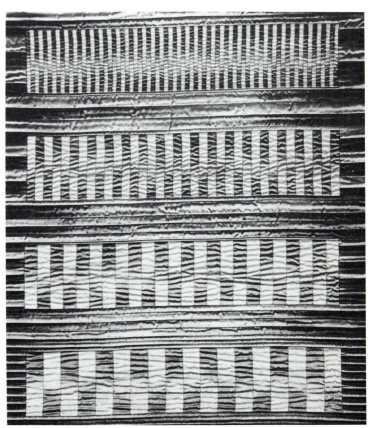

(b) Quilted hanging, air-brushed on satin acetate using disperse dyes, by Diana Harrison

interesting when different colours are splattered on top of each other (Fig. 9.15).

The air-brush is a finer tool altogether. It is about the size and shape of a large fountain pen. Like the tjanting (the tool used in batik) it has a small reservoir that holds the dye. When the air-brush is connected to a compressor or canister of compressed air a small lever can be pressed which releases a very fine spray (see Fig. 9.13).

SPRAYING WITH PIGMENTS

Although there are many dyes that can be used on paper since they do not require fixing, it is a limited number that are suitable for spraying on to cloth. Procion MX dyes are suitable for cellulosic fibres, acids for wool and silk, and disperse dyes for some synthetics (see Fig. 9.14).

Pigments are extremely easy to use with an air-brush or spray gun, as they need only be mixed with their relevant binder and diluted with water. They should be diluted to the consistency of single cream, in the following way:

1. Mix the pigment with the binder in the normal proportions, taking note of two things: (a) that the eventual dilution with

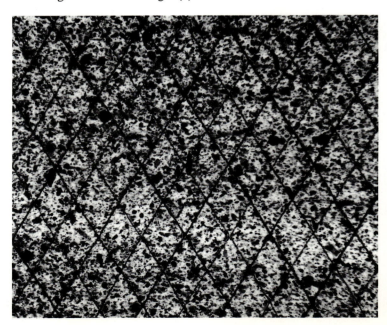

Fig. 9.15 Different colours can be used to build up a multicoloured texture by being flicked on top of each other. Sample by Diana Harrison

water will increase the volume (so mix up less pigment and binder than normal); and (b) decrease the intensity of the colour (so mix up a strong version of the colour you eventually intend to use, i.e. for a pink, start with a red, etc. A primary, or strong colour can be brought back to its original intensity during spraying by building it up in layers.)

2. Add cold water, drop by drop, to the mixture, stirring energetically to prevent curdling.
3. When the mixture is the consistency of thin cream, strain it through a fine cloth (e.g. a piece of fine screen mesh).
4. Test the colour by spraying it over a small area on a piece of cloth. Mask the area first with masking tape, so that when you spray you produce an even area of colour which will be against a white ground when the tape is removed.

The required colour should be built up without soaking the cloth. If the cloth does appear to be wet this indicates that the intensity of the colour is too weak. A stronger colour must be mixed up that can be applied in a thinner layer, and therefore will not saturate the fabric. (Dye that bleeds on the sample will also bleed underneath stencils that may be used on the finished work.)

If you have to make adjustments to the colour, remember that thick must never be added to thin: if the colour is to be strengthened, a new colour/binder mixture must be made, and the diluted solution added to it. The new mixture must then be strained.

SPRAYING WITH DISPERSE DYES

Satin is a fabric that, like silk, seems ideally suited to the air-brush or spray gun. The soft shaded effects produced with the air-brush ideally complement the surface sheen of satin. Most commonly available satins today are acetates, and it is these that are suitable for disperse dyes.

Pigments can be sprayed onto satin, and because of their composition, sit on the surface of the cloth and slightly dull its shine. This makes an interesting contrast between matt and shiny. Pigments sprayed onto satin are 'fast' provided that the fabric can be fixed by baking or ironing at a temperature of 120–150 °C (250–300 °F). (As hot as the fabric will stand, if ironing.)

If, however, an all-over shiny surface is required, disperse dyes should be used, as they do not 'disguise' the surface of the fabric. The following recipe for printing disperse dyes can be used, the amount of thickening reduced as required.

Printing recipe for disperse dyes (reduce thickener for spraying)
You will need:

x grams	dyestuff to the maximum specified by supplier
250–300 ml	water
600 ml	thickener (reduce as required to form a milk-like consistency)
10 g	Resist Salt L
20 ml	perminal KB

Suitable thickeners include Manutex RS and Thickening 301, mixed to suppliers' instructions or those outlined previously.

Procedure

1. Set aside a little of the water, and dissolve the Resist Salt L in it. Also add the Perminal KB.
2. Paste up the dyestuff in a little of the water. Heat the rest but do not boil it, and add it to the dye-paste, dissolving it completely (strain if necessary).
3. Add the Perminal KB and Resist Salt L solution to thickener.
4. Stir in the dye solution. Fabrics sprayed or painted with this solution require fixing by steaming (see Ch. 6, p. 161).

EFFECTS AND PROCEDURES

Spray guns and air-brushes are delicate pieces of equipment, and must be treated with respect. They should be sprayed through the cold water each time the colour is changed, and at intervals to prevent clogging. If pigments are being used, the gun should not be left standing filled with pigment for more than about 4–5 minutes. A flush through with water will clear pigment that remains in the gun, and the water will eventually run clear. It is a good idea, when cleaning, to spray on to a piece of white paper, as any residue of colour that is left will show up clearly, indicating that the gun is not perfectly clean.

When attempting to spray a large even area of colour, the spray gun must be held well above the work, and the nozzle adjusted to produce a broad, but fine spray. The nozzle can be opened up fully, but checks should be maintained on the coarseness of the spray, as if a darkish colour is being used, it will read as a mass of tiny dots, and not as a fine spray.

When spraying, the gun must always be kept moving. A piece of paper should be placed adjacent to the work, and the spray started and finished on the paper. The gun must then be moved quickly and smoothly across the fabric at a height that will produce the required coverage and depth of colour. This will avoid dark areas of colour forming at the beginning and end of spraying.

The dark pools of colour that will result if the spray gun is held still for a moment means that colour must be built up in sweeping layers. This characteristic means that overlays of different colours can be used. It also means that pools of colour can be deliberately made, and used as part of a design, forming a build-up of soft blobs.

If the nozzle of the gun is actually held *on* the cloth, and short bursts of dye pressed out, 'spiders' will occur, formed by small spreading pools of colour which have been forced through the slightly serrated end of the nozzle which is resting on the cloth. These can form colourful 'constellations' if waxed over, and the background subsequently dyed or sprayed in a darker colour.

Many different effects can be created by spraying. The fabric can be pleated, and sprayed along the pleats. Multiple folds in different directions will result in tartans and checks. The fabric can also be crumpled, and sprayed, resulting in *trompe-l'oeil* creases when it is ironed flat. Lace and other delicate open weave fabrics can be sprayed through, creating textures and patterns that can be used to good effect with theatrical costumes. Imitation brocades can be created in the same way, using a denser build-up of layers of colour and a variety of stencils (Fig. 9.16).

The spray, even from a small air-brush, is far-reaching. Being so fine it is carried on the air, and settles far beyond the immediate range of the gun. This means that a safety mask must be worn to avoid breathing any dye particles, and that every area on the cloth that is not to be coloured should be covered. In graphic work, a low-tack transparent masking film is used to protect areas that are not to be coloured. Laid in position over a design, with shapes cut away with a knife, it forms a stencil through which to spray. Unfortunately, it is difficult to use this film ('Frisk' film) on fabric. However, many other stencils can be used. Cartridge paper or card are suitable, and masking tape is extremely useful.

Stencils

When using paper for a stencil there is always a danger that the force of the air from the spray gun will lift the paper and allow the dye to get underneath. This is particularly likely if the spray gun is held close to the cloth and the spray directed

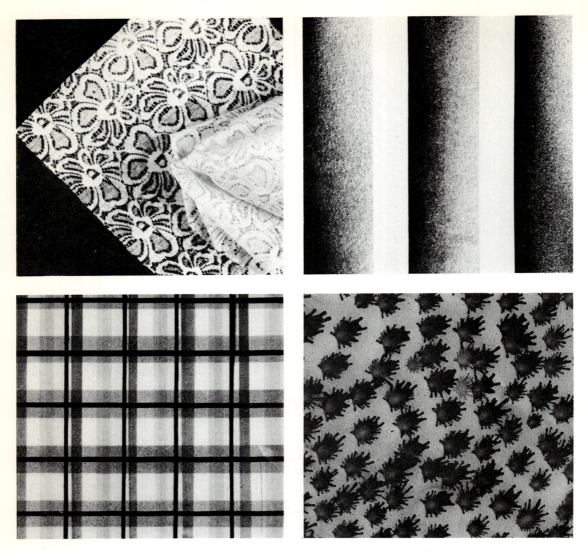

Fig. 9.16 Air-brush effects.
'Lace'
'Pillars'
'Tartans'
'Space invaders'

horizontally. The spray gun should be held well above the work, and moved in sweeping movements over the edge being sprayed, i.e. with the spray gun being held over the stencil and the spray directed towards the cloth. If a small shape is being sprayed, the gun or air-brush should be held as vertical as possible over the shape so that the spray is directed downwards, and there is less danger of it getting under the stencil.

To further lessen the likelihood of bleeding, weights can be placed on the stencil or, if hard, straight edges are being

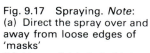

Fig. 9.17

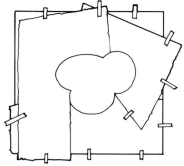

Fig. 9.18

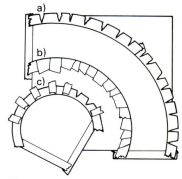

Fig. 9.19

Fig. 9.17   Spraying. *Note*:
(a) Direct the spray over and
away from loose edges of
'masks'
(b) Use weights to hold down
lightweight masking materials
(c) Use tape to secure edges of
masks wherever practical

Fig. 9.18   Use several small
pieces of paper to form one large
shape, as they will not buckle so
easily as one large one

Fig. 9.19   Masking around
shapes:
(a) The tape should be cut and
opened out around outside curves
(b) Cut and overlapped around
inside curves
(c) Cover nicks and cuts in the
tape with small pieces of tape

sprayed, lines of masking tape can be used to form part of the stencil, and to hold it down on the cloth (see Fig. 9.17).

If objects are being used as 'negative stencils' (i.e. being sprayed *around*) they should be as flat as possible, otherwise a distorted image will result due to the angle at which the spray hits the cloth, having been deflected by the object.

Objects, or small shapes that are being sprayed around, should be attached to the fabric with small pieces of double-sided tape, as care must be taken to keep them flat.

If a large shape is cut out of a piece of paper which is to serve as a stencil, the remaining area around the shape tends to buckle, and it is difficult to keep it lying flat. In some cases it is a good idea to form one large shape from several pieces of paper, each attached to the cloth individually, or to use a special type of masking paper that can be ironed to the cloth (see Fig. 9.18).

In the fashion industry, a gummed paper is used to back fabrics that would otherwise be too fine to cut out accurately. The paper stiffens fabric such as chiffon, making it more easy to handle. This paper can be used by the textile printer as a stencil. Shapes are cut out of it, and the paper or the shape is ironed to the cloth with a *warm* iron.

As with any stencil, the paper must not be allowed to become soaked with dye. Once droplets of dye collect around the edges of the stencil there is danger of bleeding. It also signifies that the edge of the cloth around the stencil may be getting too wet. Dye can still bleed under a stencil even if it is gummed to the cloth. Small drops or a fine spray of colour can be quickly blotted off the stencil, and pose no problem.

Masking tape is the ideal stencil material as it can be used to secure newsprint and form a straight or curved edge around shapes (see Figs 9.19 and 9.20; see also Fig. 5.39). When

237

masking around a curved shape, cuts should be made in the tape at intervals to enable it to be spread around curves. Around an outside curve, the cuts will open out and spread the tape, while around an inside curve the cuts in the tape will overlap. Obviously, it is vital before spraying, to cover any cuts left open in the tape, with further pieces of tape.

Black pigment is a good 'stencil' to use with spraying techniques. As printed black pigment is so dense and solid a fine spray can be sprayed up to, and over, the pigment without leaving a mark. It is particularly successful on heavier

Fig. 9.20 Printed, masked, and sprayed panel, by Bridget Miles

Fig. 9.21 'Rainbow crystals', sprayed and printed fabric by Jane Kidd

Fig. 9.22   Illusory 3-D effects
produced by spraying fabric by
Jane Kidd

fabrics such as cotton sateen (Fig. 9.20). This means that on a
black-and-white print, selected areas can be sprayed or
splattered without the need for time-consuming masking with
paper and tape.

   The black pigment must, however, be fixed before the
more liquid colour is sprayed on, or small water marks will
occur. The fabric can be fixed by ironing, and by doing so
will not need to be removed from the table between printing
and spraying.

   Sprayed black pigment can produce convincing illusory
three-dimensional effects, especially when the article that has
been sprayed is later quilted or stuffed (Fig. 9.21).

   As a technique, fabric spraying is very versatile. It can be
used with many other techniques, including batik and tie-dye,
and its softness is a good foil to the hard effects produced by
screen printing (Fig. 9.22).

UK Suppliers

SCREEN PRINTING: EQUIPMENT AND MATERIALS

Screens
1. Screen Process Supplies Limited, 24 Parsons Green Lane, London, SW6 4HS
2. Pronk Davis & Rusby, 90–96 Brewery Road London, N7 9PD

Materials only
3. A. J. Purdy & Co. Limited, 248 Lea Bridge Road, Leyton, London, E10

Tables and general equipment, including table coverings
4. Link Cable Limited, Windmill Street, Macclesfield, Cheshire, SK11 7HS
5. Pronk Davis & Rusby (general equipment), 90–96 Brewery Road, London, N7 9PD

Screen mesh
6. Screen Process Supplies Limited, 24 Parsons Green Lane, London, SW6 4HS
7. Pronk Davis & Rusby, 90–96 Brewery Road London, N7 9PD

Screen coatings and sensitiser
8. Screen Process Supplies Limited, 24 Parsons Green Lane, London, SW6 4HS
9. A. J. Purdy & Co. Limited, 248 Lea Bridge Road Leyton London, E10
10. Pronk Davis & Rusby, 90–96 Brewery Road, London, N7 9PD

Tracing films (Kodatrace/Permatrace)
11. Screen Process Supplies Limited, 24 Parsons Green Lane, London, SW6 4HS
12. Pronk Davis & Rusby, 90–96 Brewery Road, London, N7 9PD

Cutting films (Stenplex Amber/Profilm)
13. Pronk Davis & Rusby, 90–96 Brewery Road, London, N7 9PD
14. Screen Process Supplies Limited, 24 Parsons Green Lane, London, SW6 4HS

'Opaque' (for use on Kodatrace)
15. Screen Process Supplies Limited, 24 Parsons Green Lane, London, SW6 4HS
16. Pronk Davis & Rusby, 90–96 Brewery Road, London, N7 9PD
17. A. J. Purdy & Co. Limited, 248 Lea Bridge Road, Leyton, London, E10

Certain opaques are available through art shops

Lithographic crayons and tusche
18. Howson Algraphy, Murray Road, Orpington, Kent

Precision grids
19. Opsec Limited, Holywell Hill, St Albans, Herts.

Heat-fix paper (for use as stencils)
20. Ozalid, Langston Road, Loughton, Essex

Newsprint and other papers
21. Wiggins Teape, Park House, 165/167 The Broadway, Wimbledon, London, SW19 1NE

Low-tack masking film ('Frisk' – film)
22. Frisk Products, Unit 4, Franthorne Way, Bellingham Trading Estate, London, SE6
23. 'Frisk' film is also sold through general graphic and art supply shops

Table gums
24. Screen Process Supplies Limited, 24 Parsons Green Lane, London, SW6 4HS

Pigments (for printing)
25. Durham Chemicals, 55–57 Glengall Road, London, SE15 6NQ
26. Polyprint Limited, 815 Lisburn Road, Belfast, BT9 7GX

Oil- and vinyl-based printing inks
27. E. T. Marler Limited, 25 Deer Park Road, London, SW19 3VE
28. Screen Process Supplies Limited, 24 Parsons Green Lane, London, SW6 4HS

General chemicals
29. Thew Arnott, Wallington, Surrey

Fabrics prepared for printing – Silk
30. Pongees Limited, 184–186 Old Street, London, EC1V 9BP
31. George Veil, 63–65 Riding House Street, London, WIP 7PP

All fabrics
32. Whaleys (Bradford) Limited, Harris Court, Great Horton, Bradford W. Yorkshire, BD7 4EQ

Cotton and silk
33. McCulloch & Wallis, 25–26 Dering Street, London, W1
34. George Weil, 63–65 Riding House Street, London, WIP 7PP

Hand painting/Fabric pens
35. Hobby Tex (UK) Limited, 56 Milton Trading Estate, Milton, Abingdon, Oxon, OX14, 4RX

Spray guns and air-brushes
36. Aerograph Devilbiss, 45 Holborn Viaduct, London, EC1

Heat transfer crayons
37. 'Finart Fabricrayons', by Binney and Smith (Europe) Ltd, Ampthill Road, Bedford
    Available from 'Craftsmith' shops, and general art and craft shops

Heat transfer dyes/inks
38. e.g. 'Dispersol' from Durham Chemicals 55–57 Glengall Road London, SE15 6NQ
39. In small quantities, sold under the name 'Transcouleurs' from
    Ploton Sundries 273 Archway Road London, N6.
40. For ease of purchase when buying materials and equipment in small quantities: Dryad
    Northgates Leicester
    The company supplies a wide range of materials and equipment for use in batik, printing,
    dyeing, painting. etc.

DYEING (INCLUDING BATIK AND TIE-DYE)

Laboratory equipment (beakers, etc.)
41. Griffin & George Limited Heat Office 285 Ealing Road Wembley Middlesex, HAQ 1HJ
42. Wykeham Farrance Engineering Ltd Weston Road Slough Berkshire, SL1 4HW

Small-scale steamers
43. Link Cable Limited Windmill Street Macclesfield Cheshire, SK11 7HS

Dyestuffs
44. Dylon International (a subsidiary of Mayborn Products Ltd) Worksy Bridge Road
    Lower Sydenham London, SE26 5HD
45. D. S. Dyes (small quantities) 46 Sussex Way Cockfosters Herts.
46. Durham Chemicals 55–57 Glengall Road London, SE15 6NQ

Gums and Thickeners: 'Thickening 301'
47. Textile Dyestuffs and Chemicals (Brighouse) Ltd. Cliffe Road Brighouse, HD6 HD

'Manutex RS 5%'
48. Alginate Industries 22 Henrietta Street London, WC2E 8NB
49. Mamerflex transfer gum 221 E. T. Master 25 Deer Park Rd London SW19 3VE

General chemical products
50. Lankro Chemicals Limited Emerson House P.O. Box 1 Eccles Manchester, M30 0BH
51. May & Baker Limited Dagenham, Essex

Waxes, tjantings, etc.
52. Dryad Ltd Northgates Leicester
53. George Veil 63–65 Riding House Street London, WIP 7PP

Gutta, applicators etc.
54. George Veil 63–65 Riding House Street London, WIP 7PP
55. Candlemakers Supplies 28 Blythe Road, London W14

Bibliography

Allen, Janet, *Colour Craft*. Hamlyn

Bernard, Barbara, *Fashion in the 60's*. Academy St Bernard

Birren, F., *Colour Psychology and Colour Therapy*. Citadel

Brigadier, Anne, *Collage: A complete guide for artists*. Pitman Publications.

Brodatz, P. *Textures*. Dover Publications.

Bruandet, Pierre, *Painting on Silk*. E P Publishing

Clarke, W., *An Introduction to Textile Printing*. Newnes-Butterworths in conjunction with ICI

Childers, Richard H. (ed.) *Air Powered: The art of the air-brush*. Random House

Day, Lewis, *Pattern design*. BT Batsford Ltd.

Dendel, E. W., *African Fabric Crafts*. David and Charles

Dyrenforth, N., Adamczewski, F. *Batik techniques*. BT Batsford Ltd.,

Edwards, Edward B., *Pattern and Design with Dynamic Symmetry*. Dover

Hillier, Bevis, and Mary Banham, *A Tonic To The Nation: The Festival of Britain 1951* Thamese Hudson.

Houston, J. *Batik with Noel Dyrenforth*, Orbis Publishing Co.,

Justeema, W. *Pattern: A historical panorama*. Elek books.

Lippard, Lucy R., *Pop Art*. Thames and Hudson

Oliver, June, *Polysmmetrics*. Tarquin Publications

Proctor, Richard, M., *The Principles of Pattern*. Van Nostrand Reinhold

Rosenblum, Robert, *Frank Stella*. Penguin Books.

Scott, G., *Transfer Printing onto Man-made Fibres*. BT Batsford Ltd.

Storey, Joyce, *The Thames and Hudson Manual of Textile Printing*. Thames and Hudson

Storey, Joyce, *The Thames and Hudson Manual to Dyes and Fabrics*. Thames and Hudson

Tuer, Andrew *Japanese Stencil Designs*. Dover

Wade, David *Geometric Patterns and Borders*. Wildwood House

Ward, Michael *Art and Design in Textiles*.

Index